TICKETS

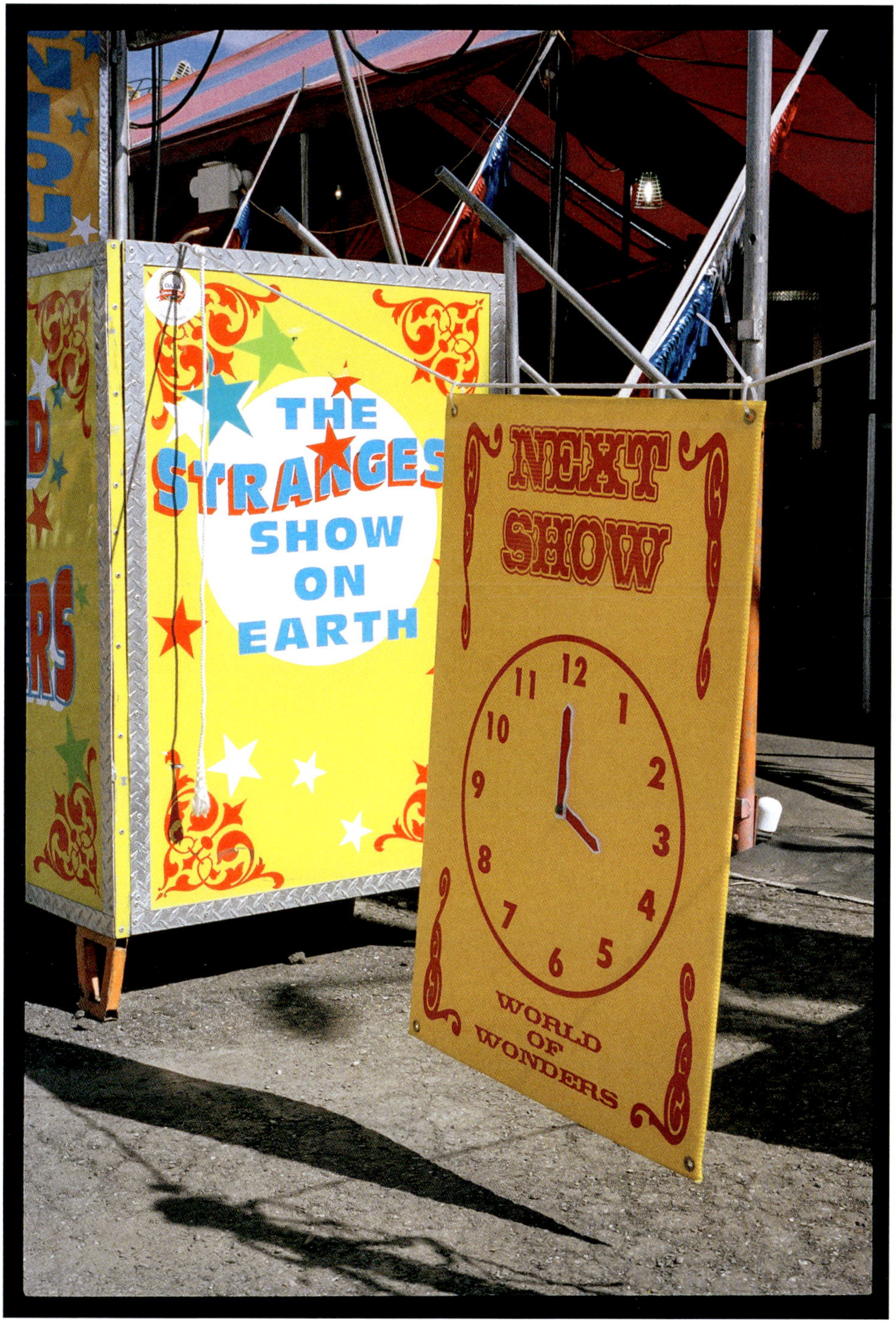
THE
STRANGEST
SHOW
ON
EARTH
NEXT
SHOW
WORLD
OF
WONDERS

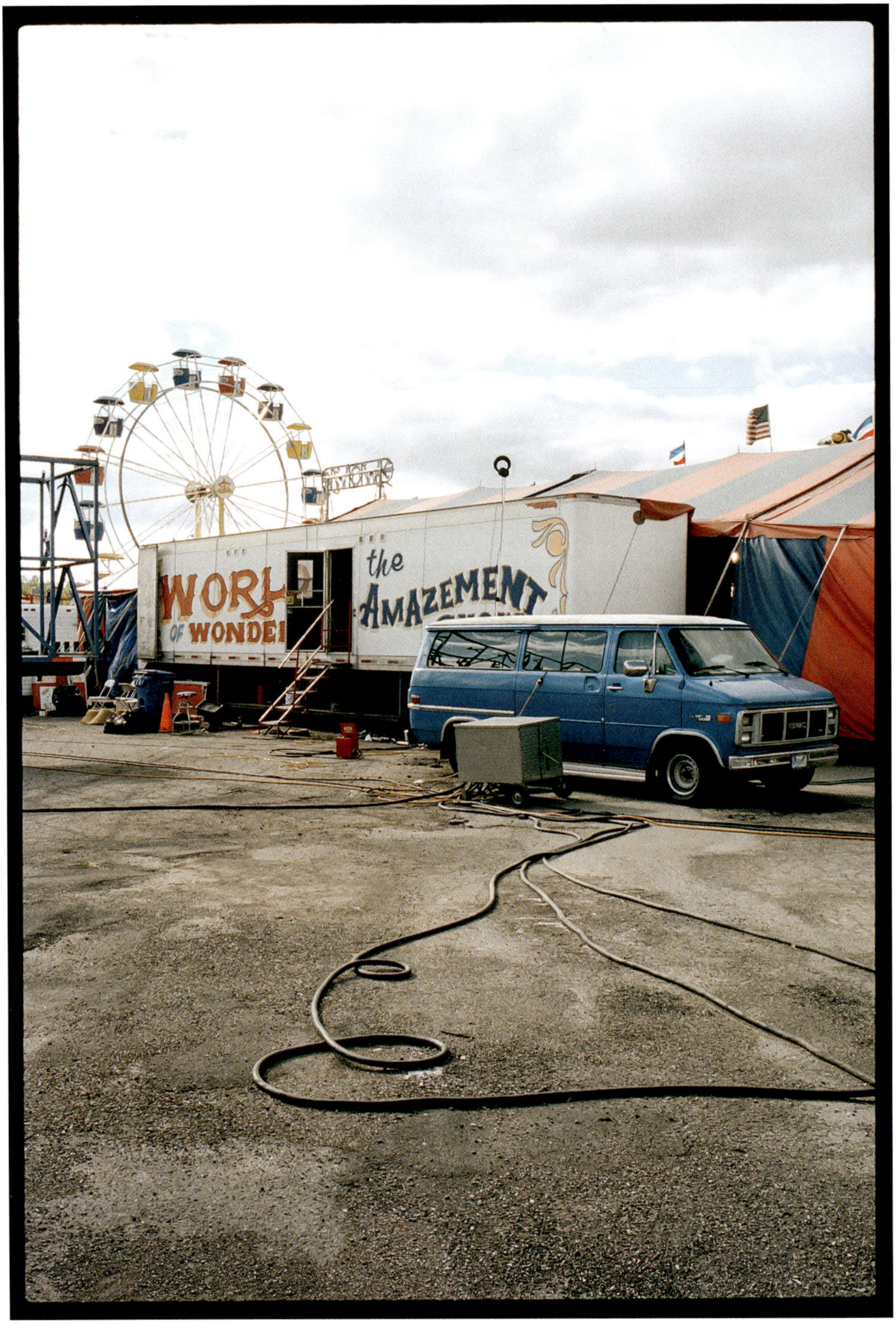
the
AMAZEMENT

TICKETS

Hunter Barnes

R|A|P
REEL ART PRESS

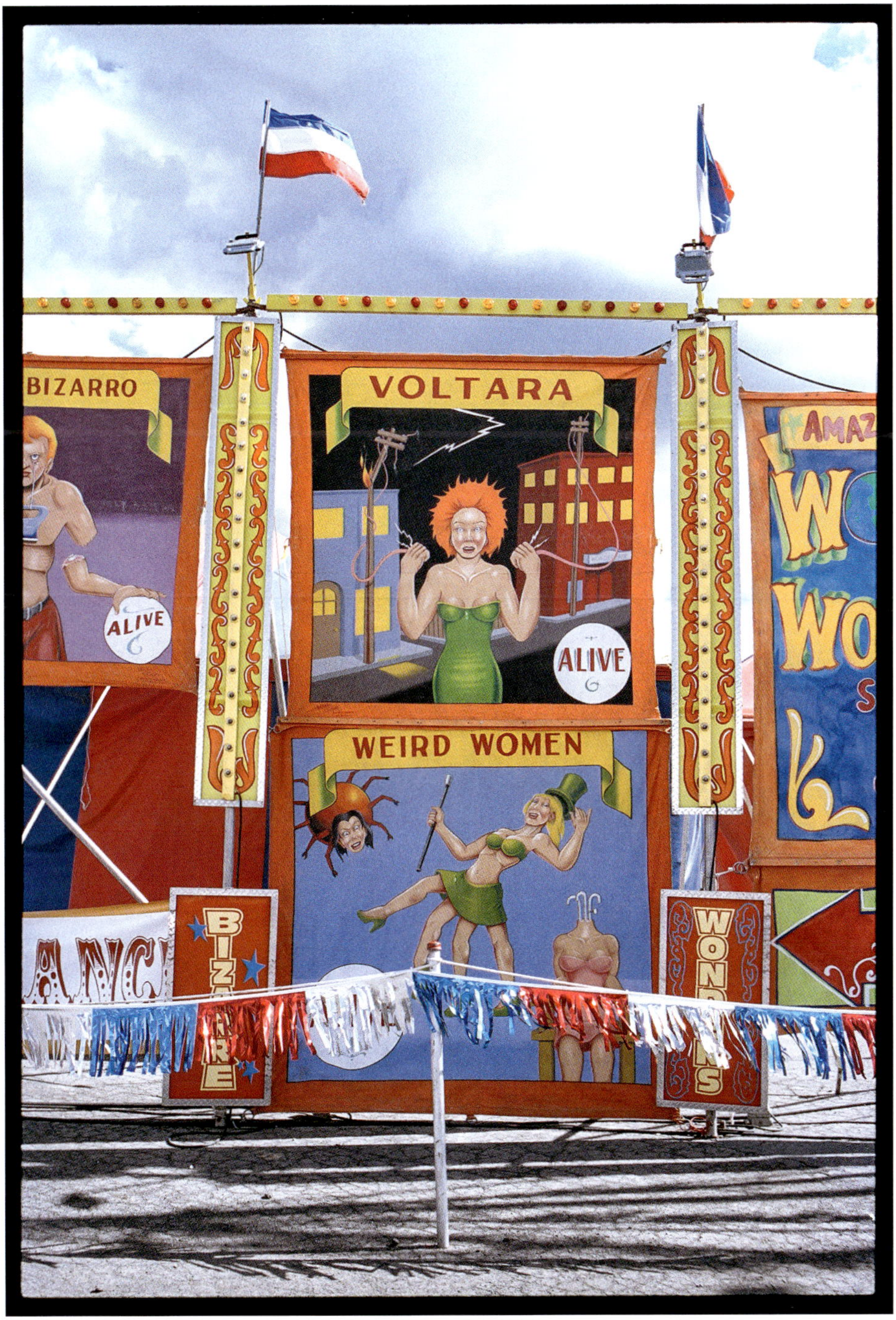
BIZARRO
ALIVE
VOLTARA
ALIVE
WEIRD WOMEN

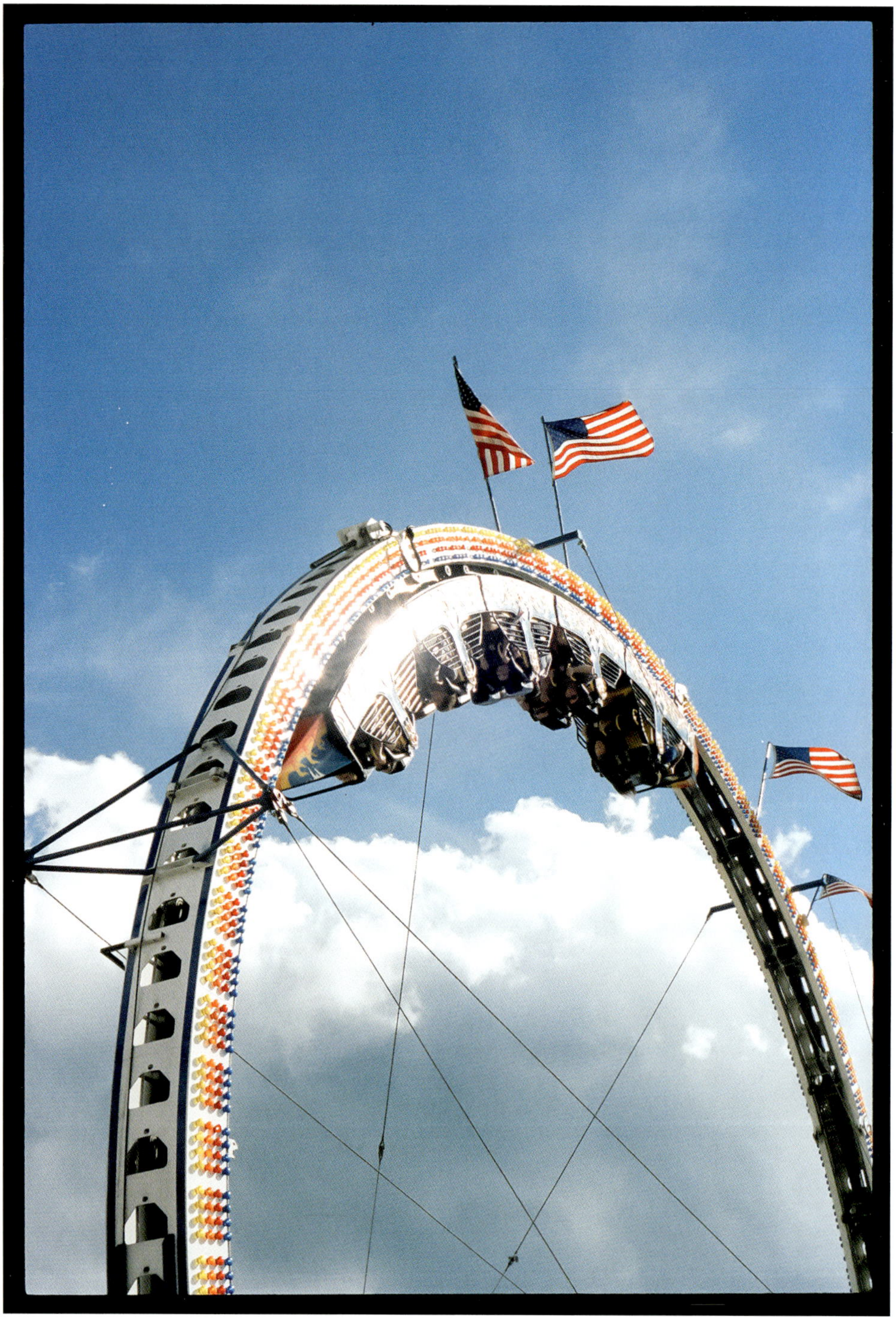

THE CARNIVAL COMES TO TOWN

A band of nomads. Roaming in open fairgrounds, spinning with color and sound.

Traveling amongst the world of wonders, entering through the banner line.

Invited to fly with the free.

Cotton candy flavors on top of the Ferris wheel's big sky.

Gamers and ride guys, sword swallowers and showmen, carnies earn a title, not stated lightly, living what it means to those who know it must be earned.

A hardworking family within, cater to the same who attend.

Fading flags are flying through children's lollipop eyes. An entrance to a magic city awaiting, that will move soon again.

Sometimes you gotta check out to check in.

We hope to see you next year.

They're with it, they're for it, and proud of it.

In a business where you never say goodbye, you'll see 'em down the line.

Hunter Barnes

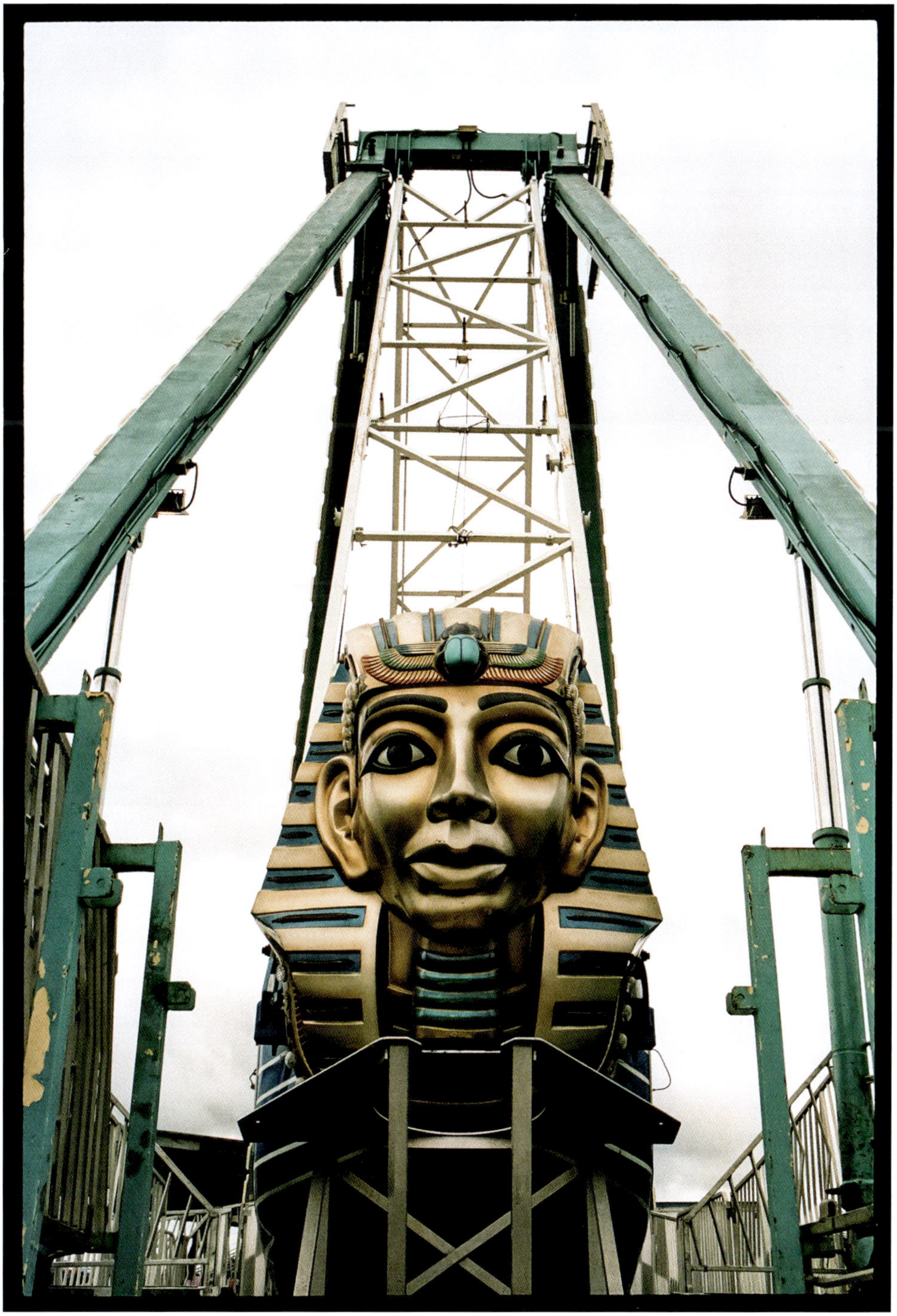

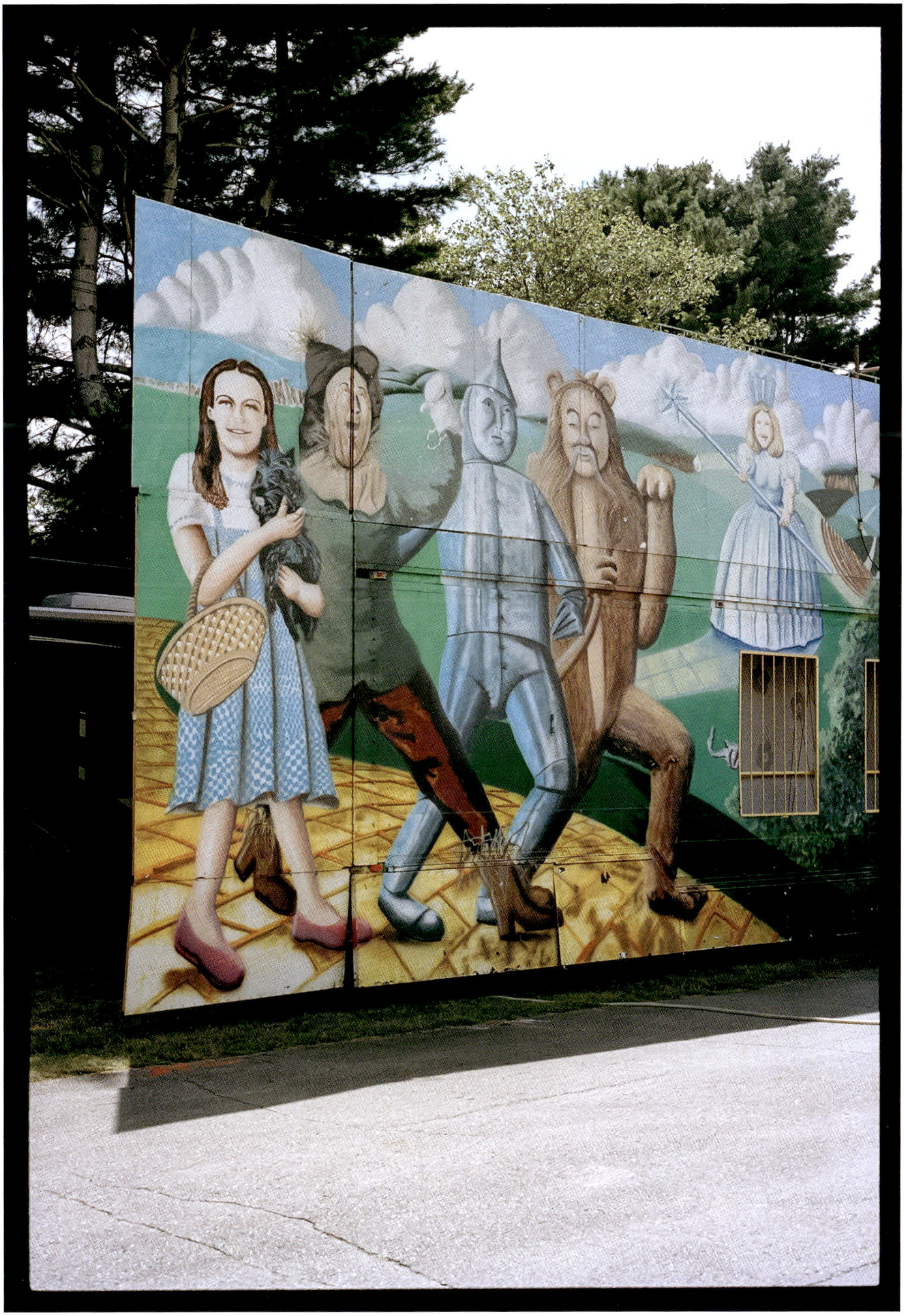

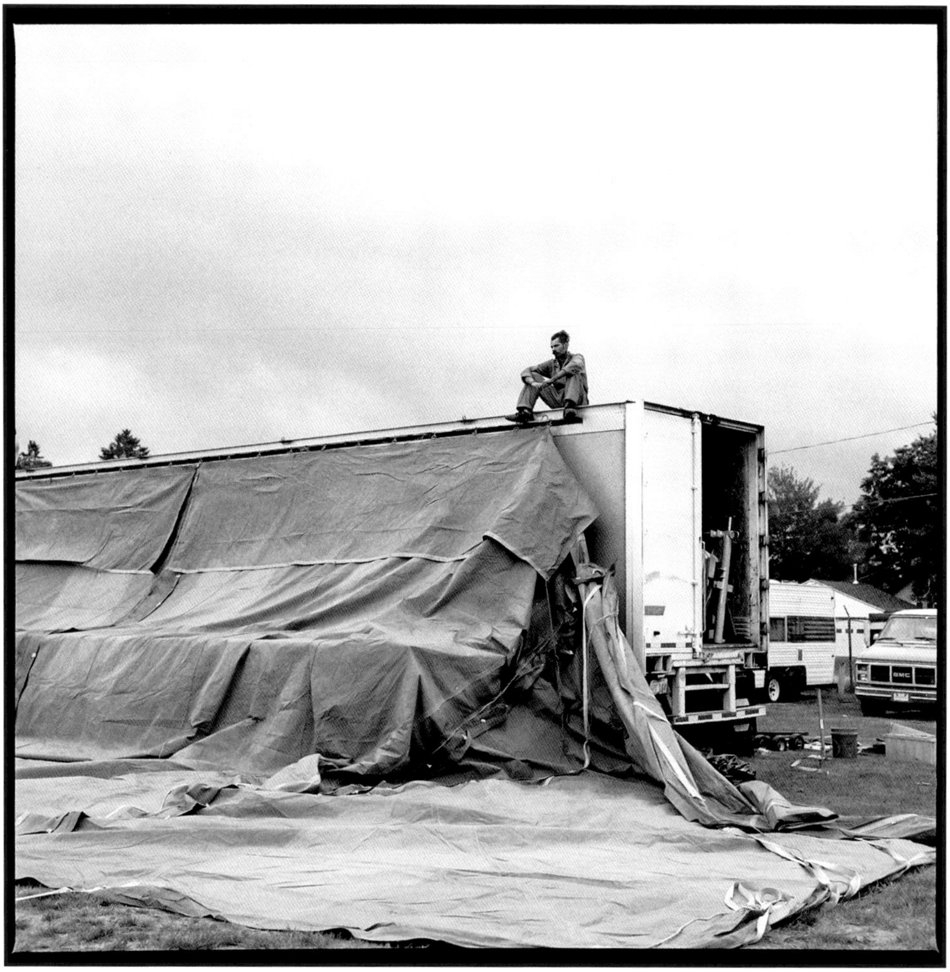

BEFORE THE SHOW

THE PHOTOGRAPHS

TICKETS

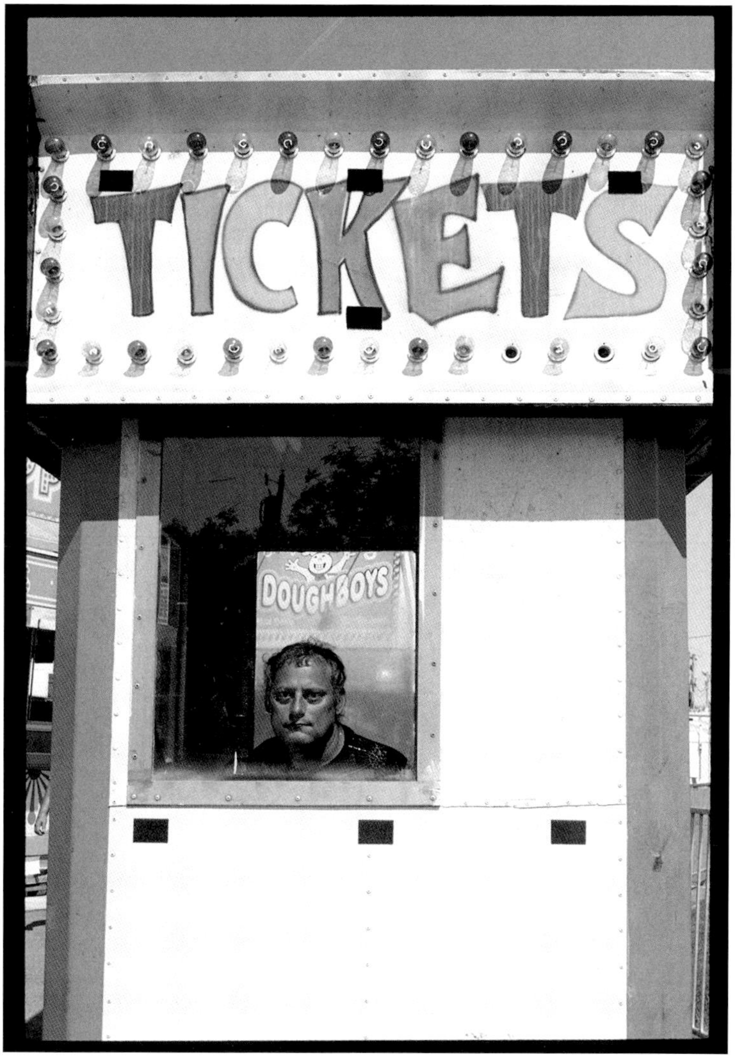
TICKETS
DOUGHBOYS

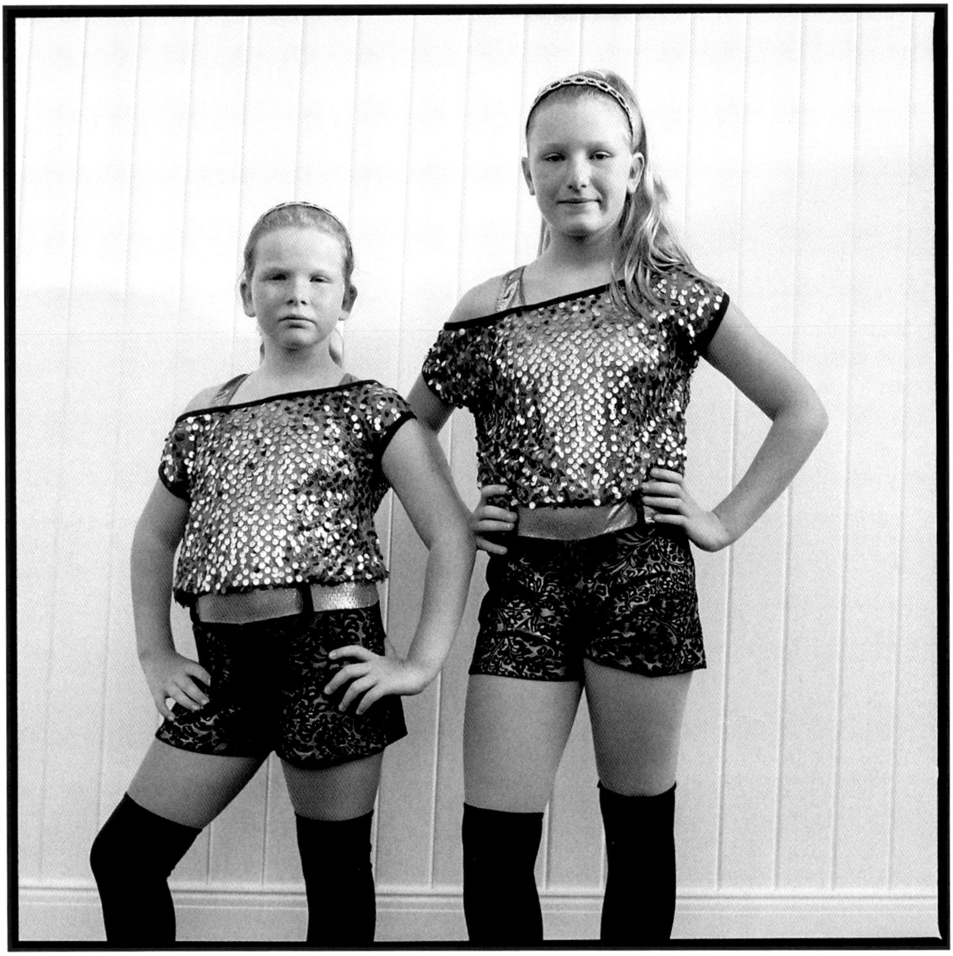

THE POMELOW SISTERS

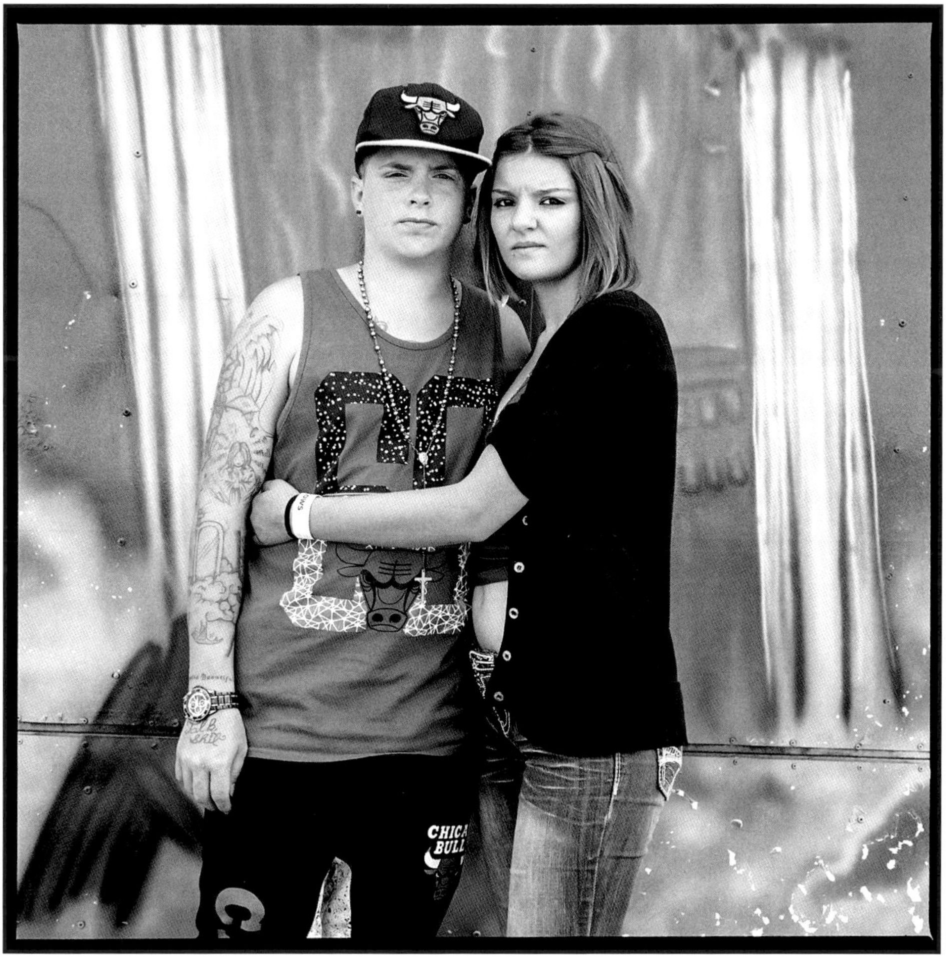

JOHN AND CASSI

KATIE AND CODIE

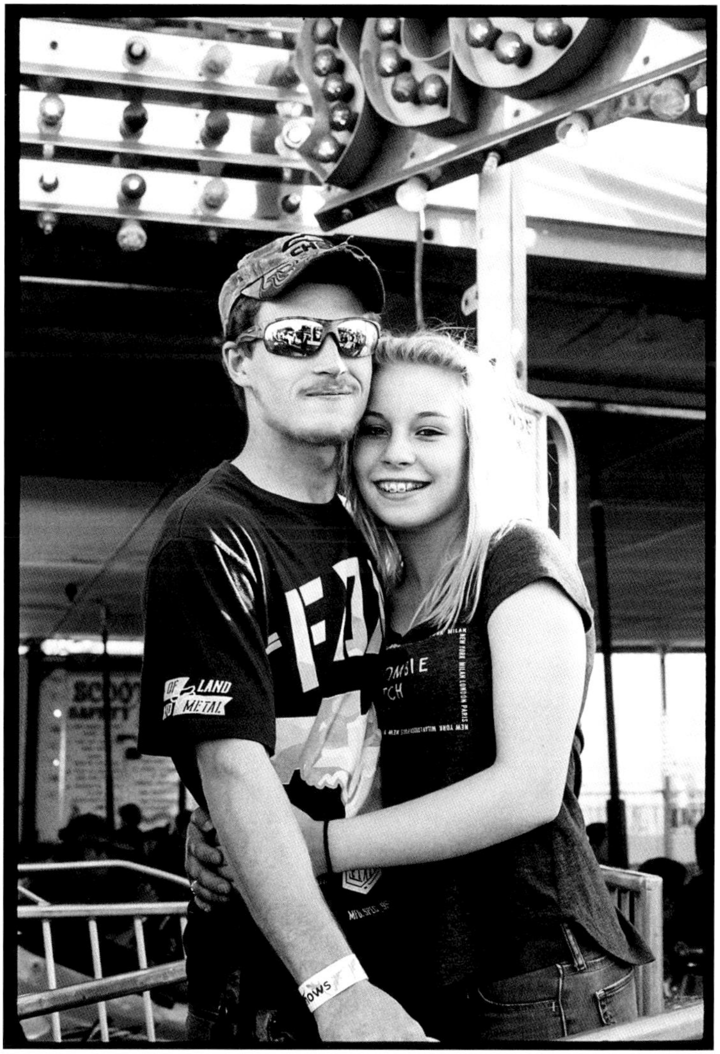

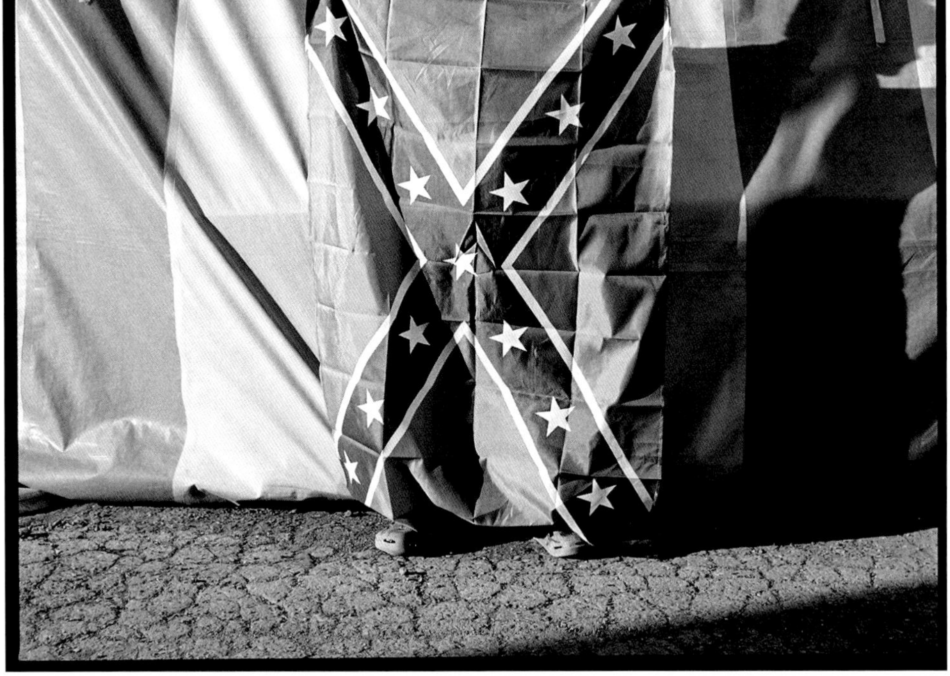

CONFEDERATE FLAG HERITAGE

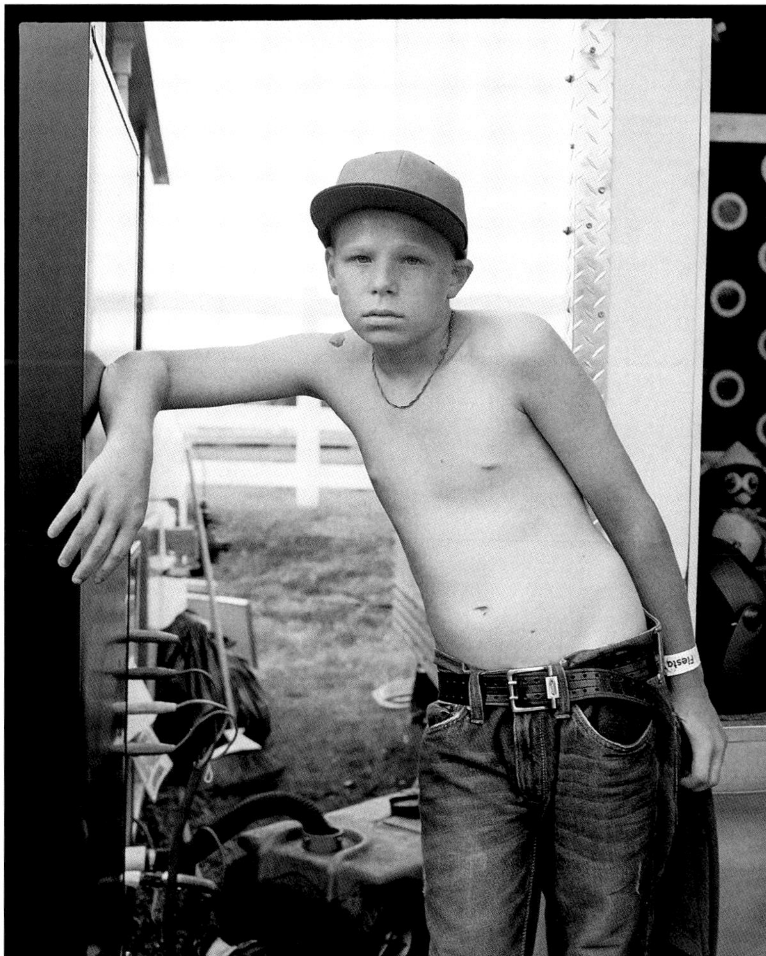

SKOWHEGAN STATE FAIR

LOCAL SHERIFF

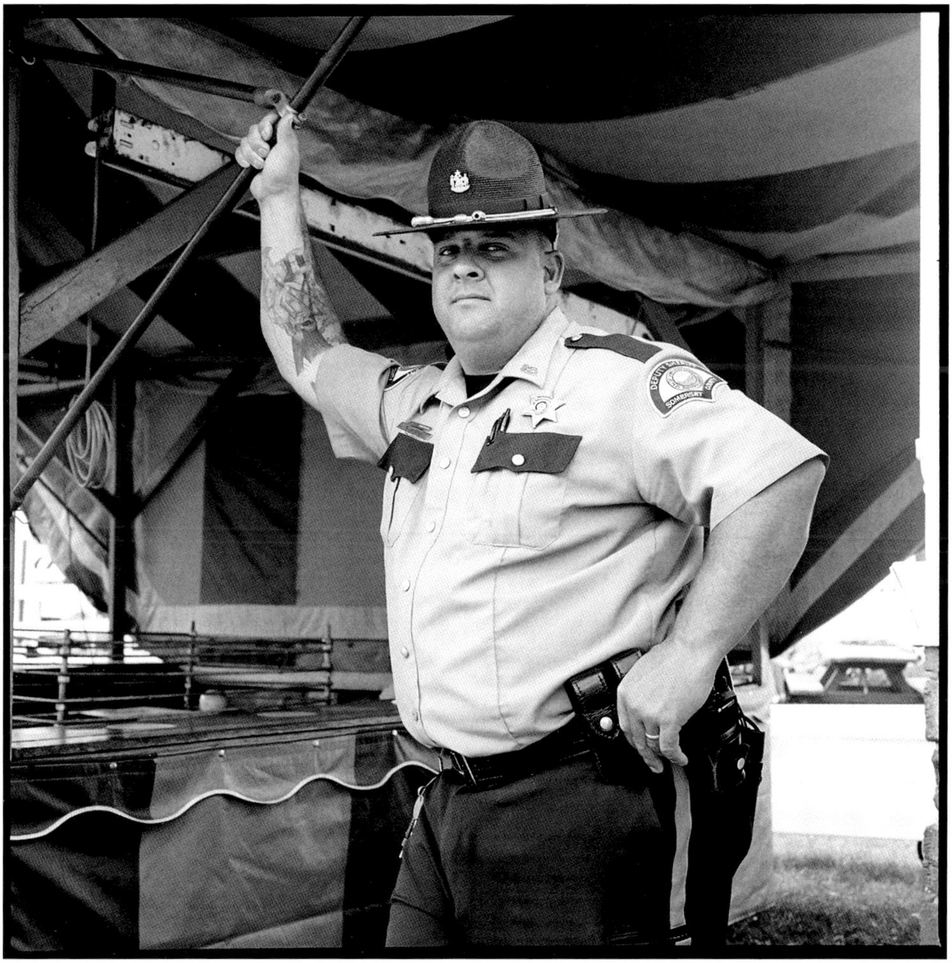
DEPUTY
SOMERSET

WARD HALL

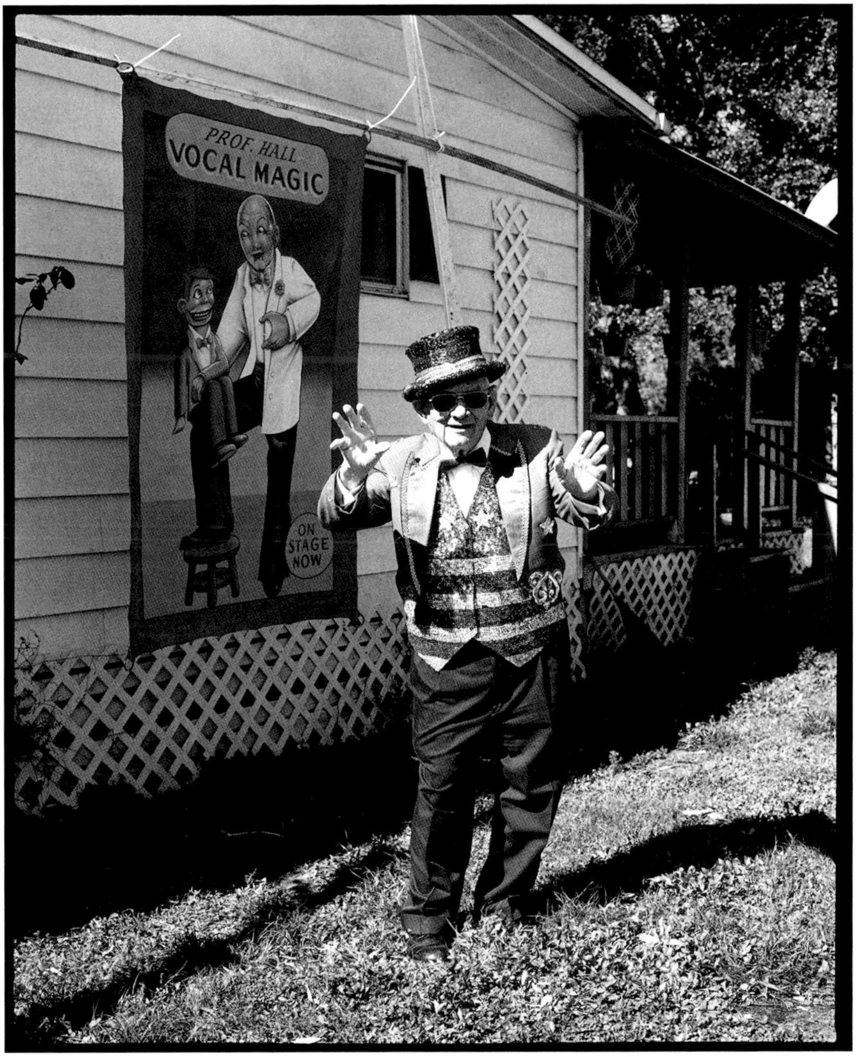
PROF. HALL
VOCAL MAGIC
ON STAGE NOW

SHOWTOWN

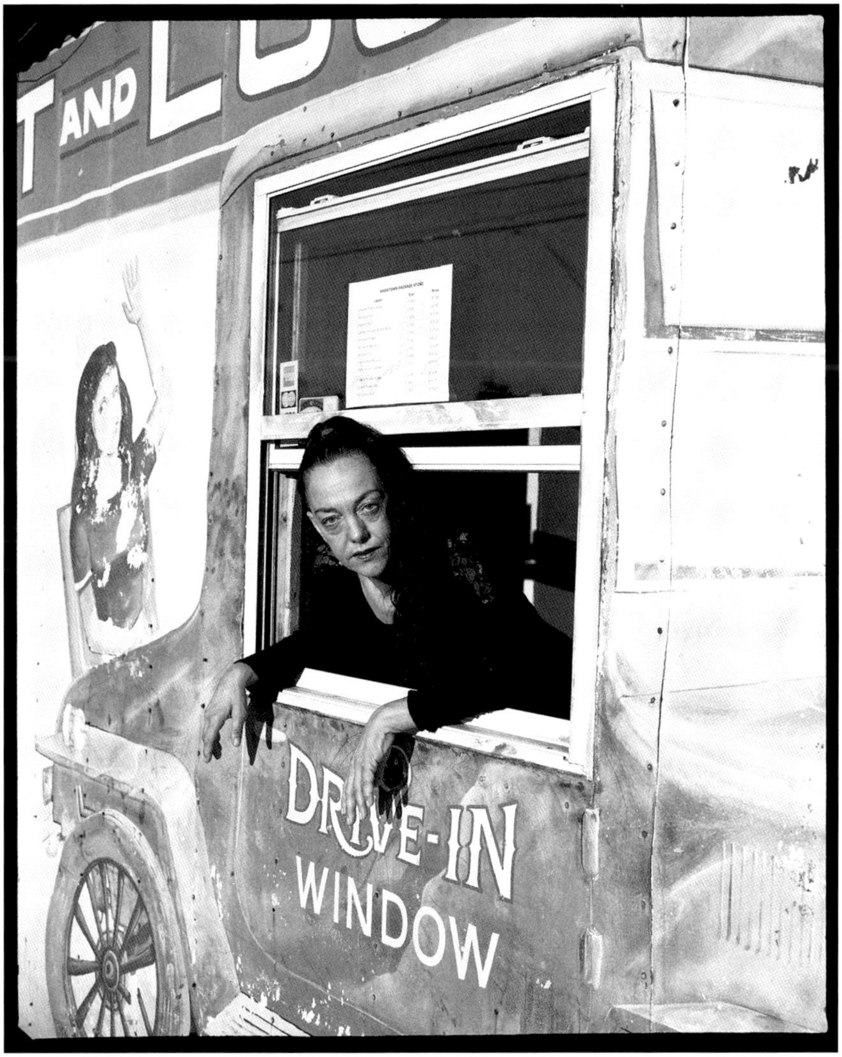

AND
DRIVE-IN
WINDOW

THE BANNER LINE

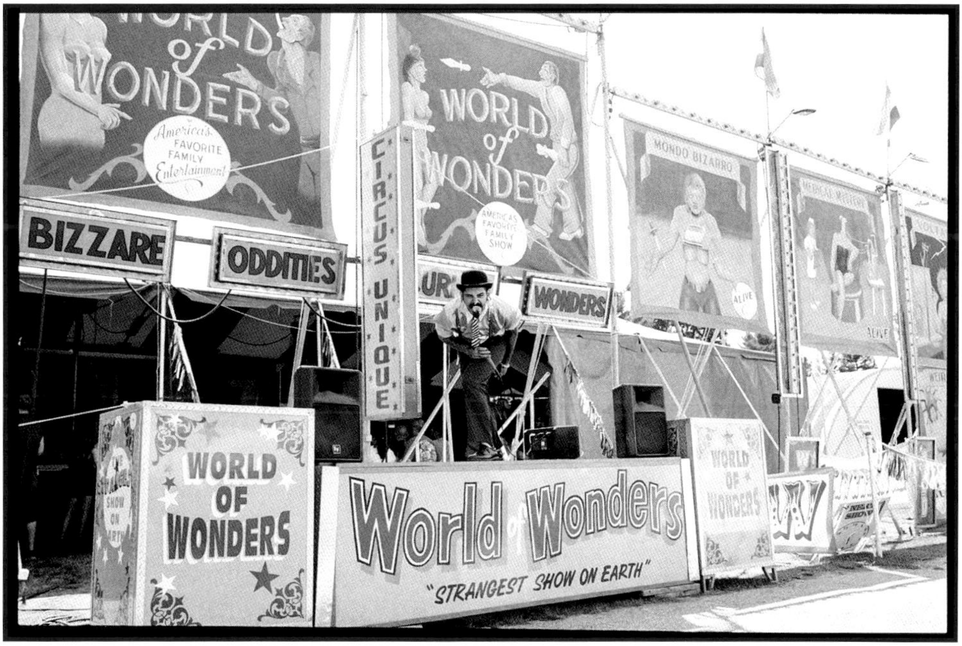
WORLD of WONDERS
America's FAVORITE FAMILY Entertainment
WORLD of WONDERS
AMERICAS FAVORITE FAMILY SHOW
CIRCUS UNIQUE
BIZZARE
ODDITIES
WONDERS
MONDO BIZARRO
ALIVE
WORLD OF WONDERS
World of Wonders
"STRANGEST SHOW ON EARTH"
WORLD OF WONDERS

SWORD SWALLOWER

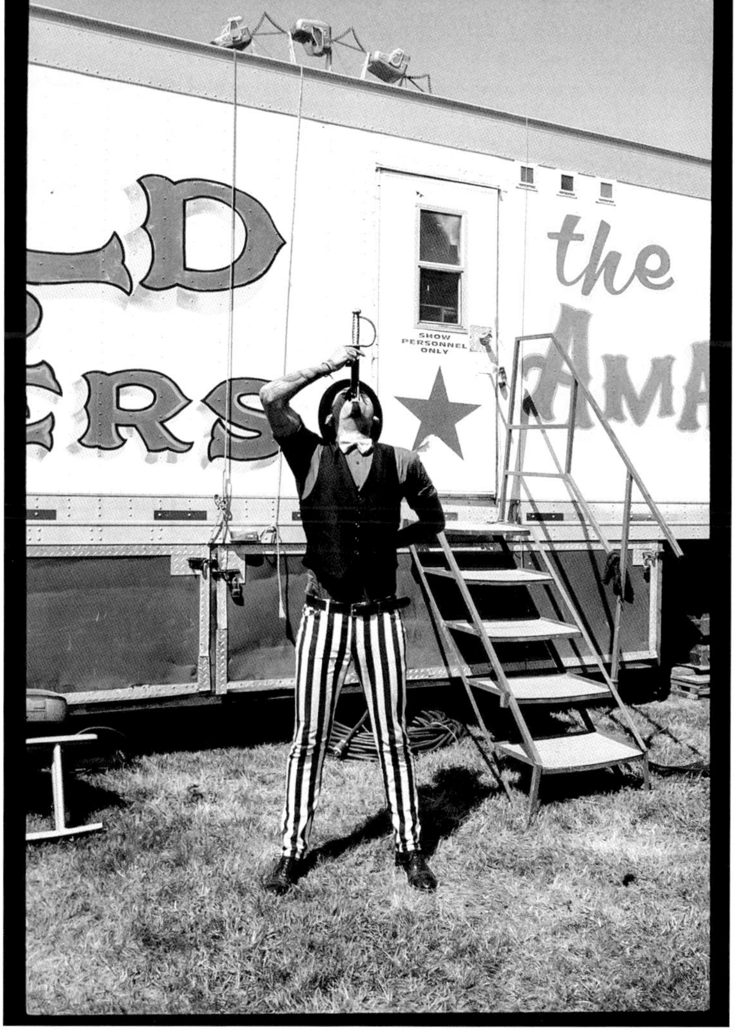
the
SHOW
PERSONNEL
ONLY

DIZZY AND TRIXIE

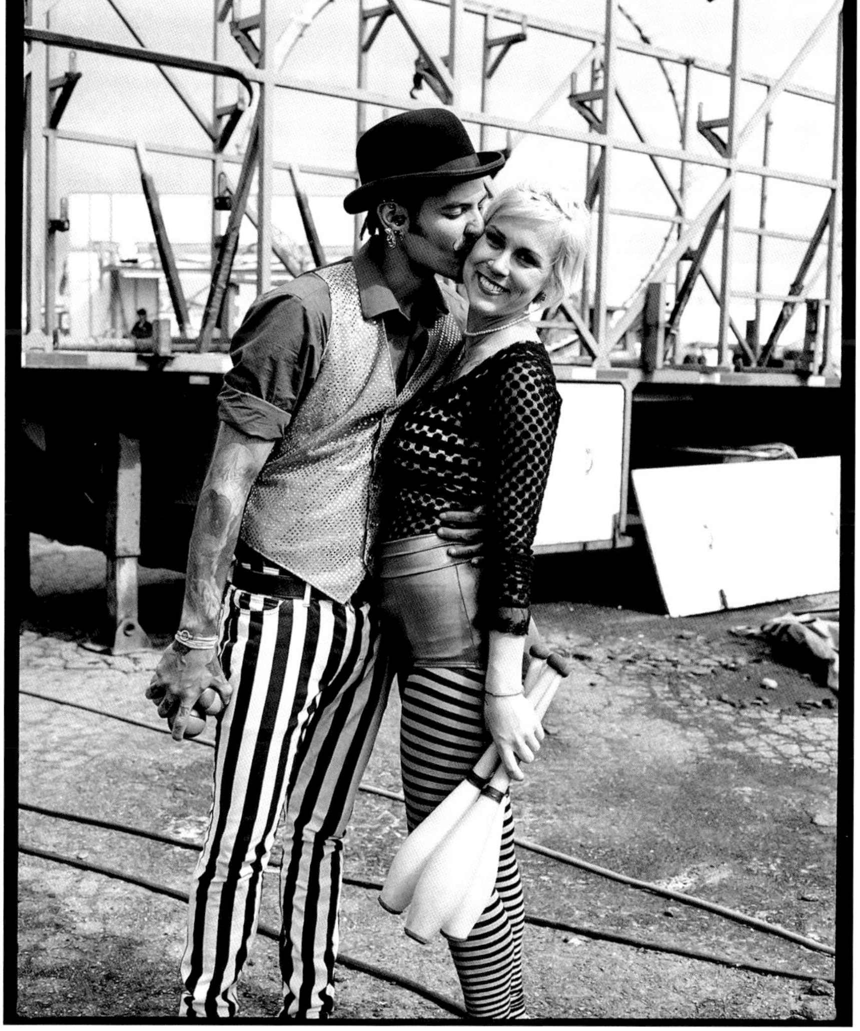

TENT CITY

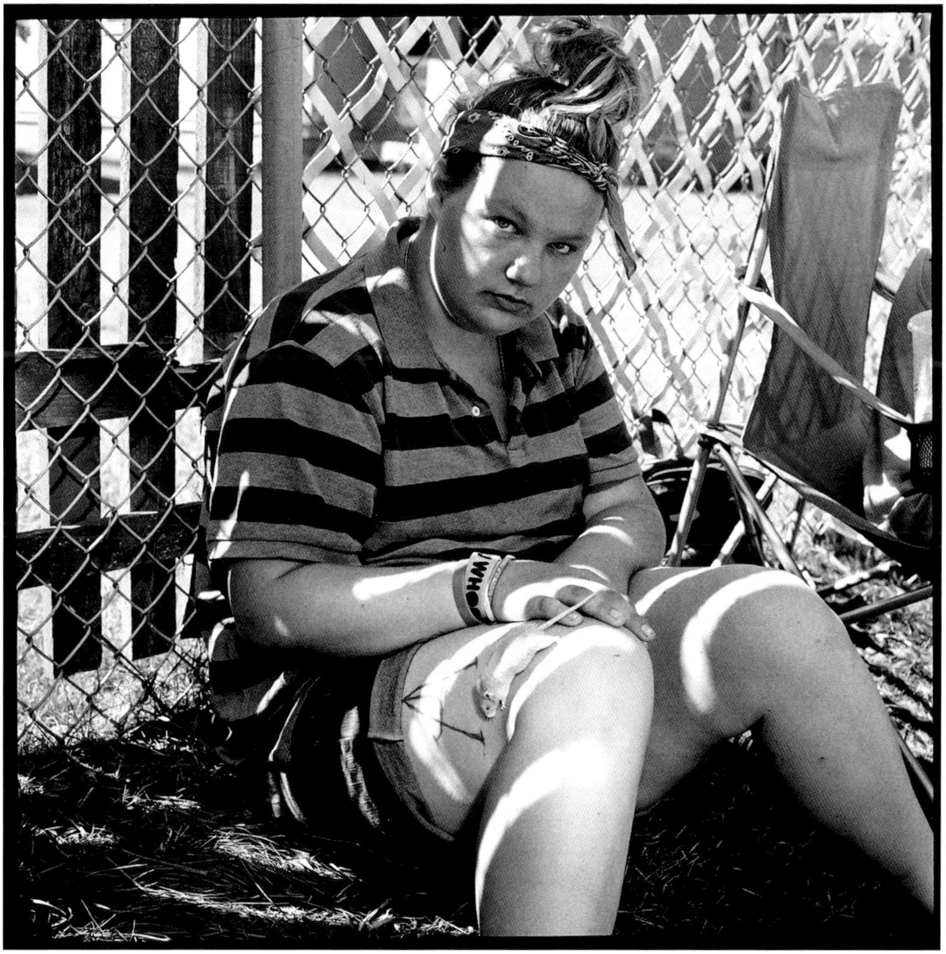

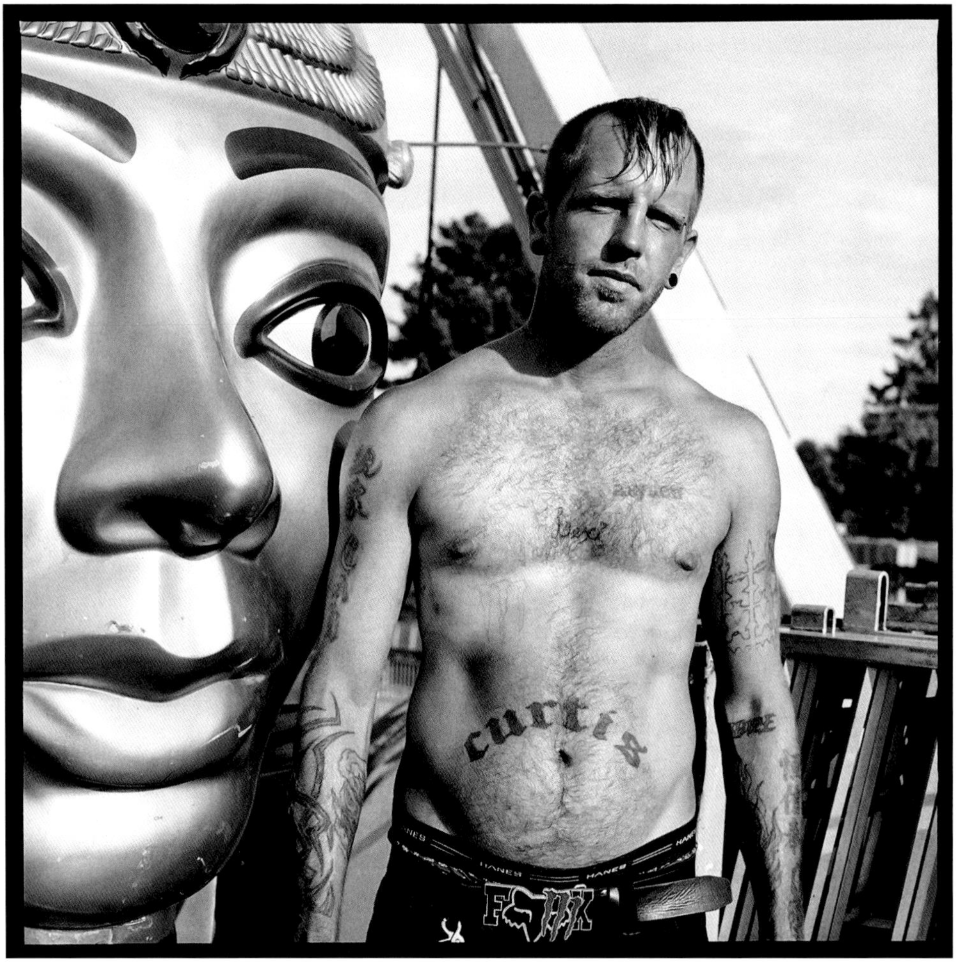

CAL

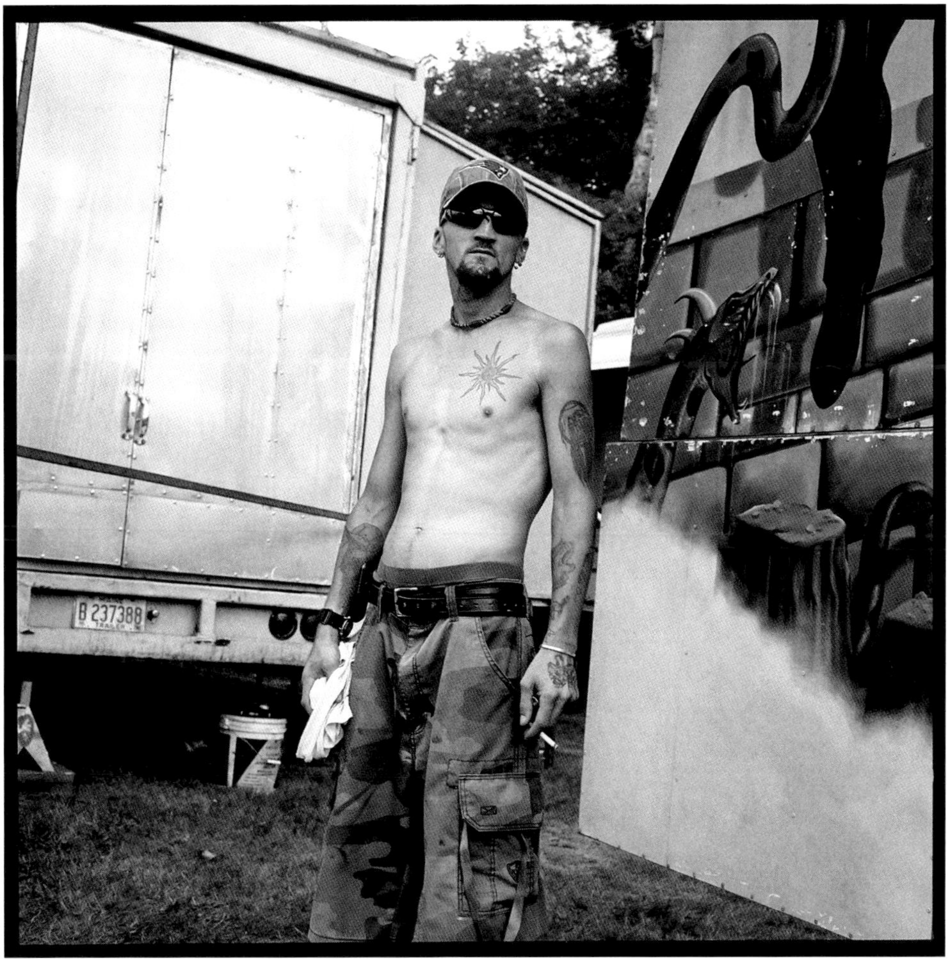

ENTRANCE TO TENT CITY

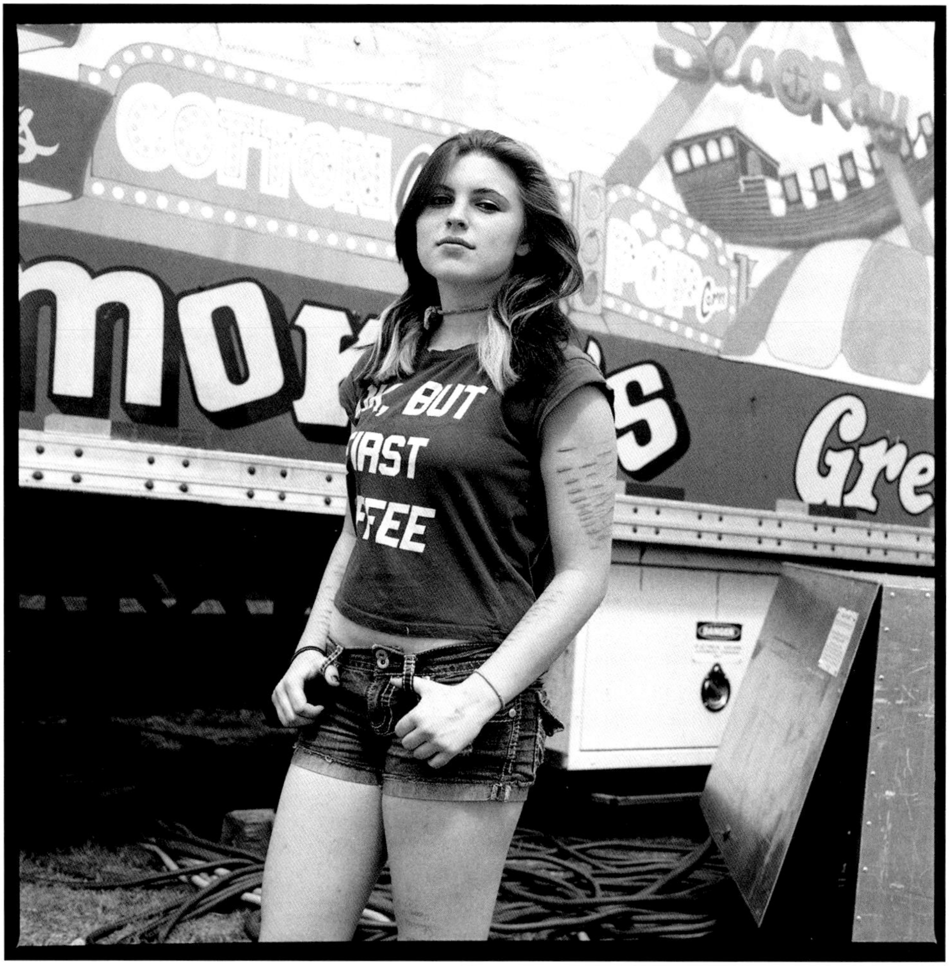

MACKENZIE

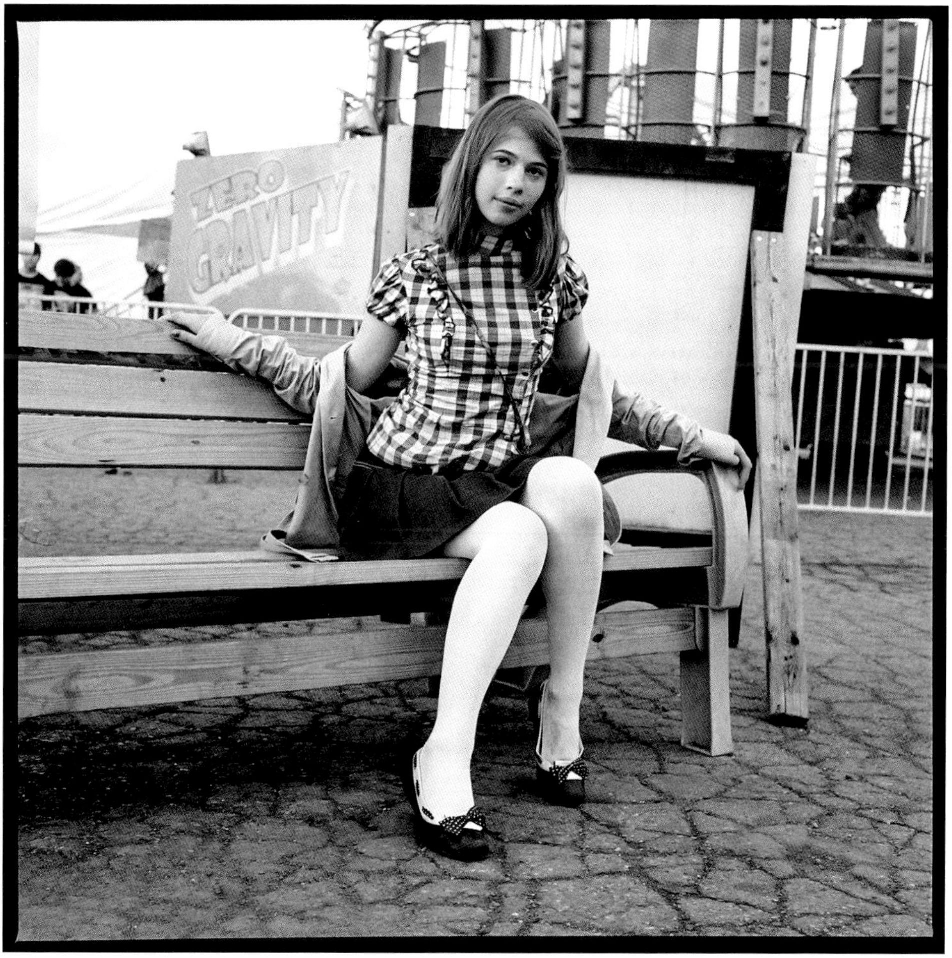

SILVIA

SEE WHAT GOD CAN DO

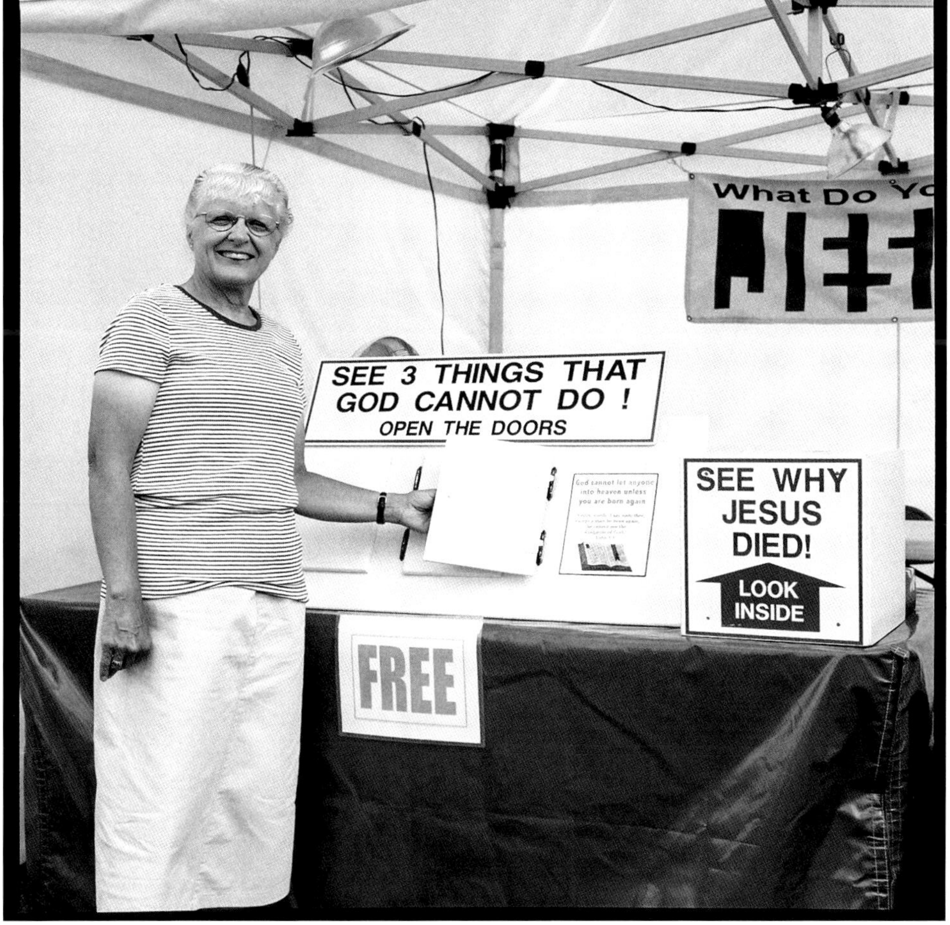
SEE 3 THINGS THAT GOD CANNOT DO !
OPEN THE DOORS
God cannot let anyone into heaven unless you are born again
SEE WHY JESUS DIED!
LOOK INSIDE
FREE

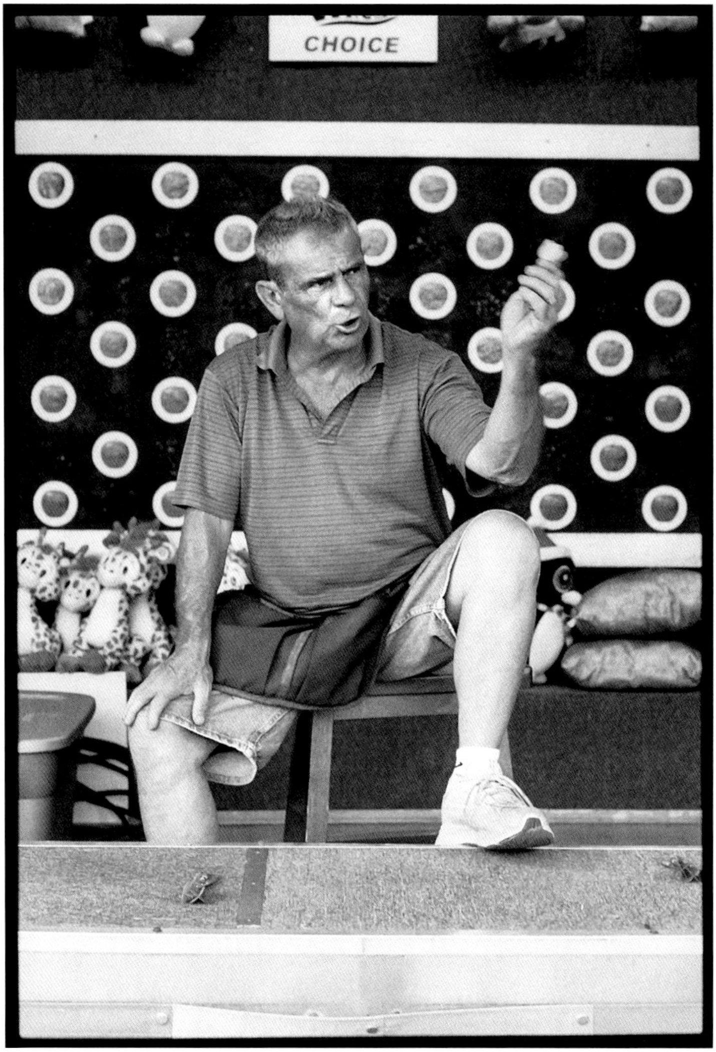

GAMER

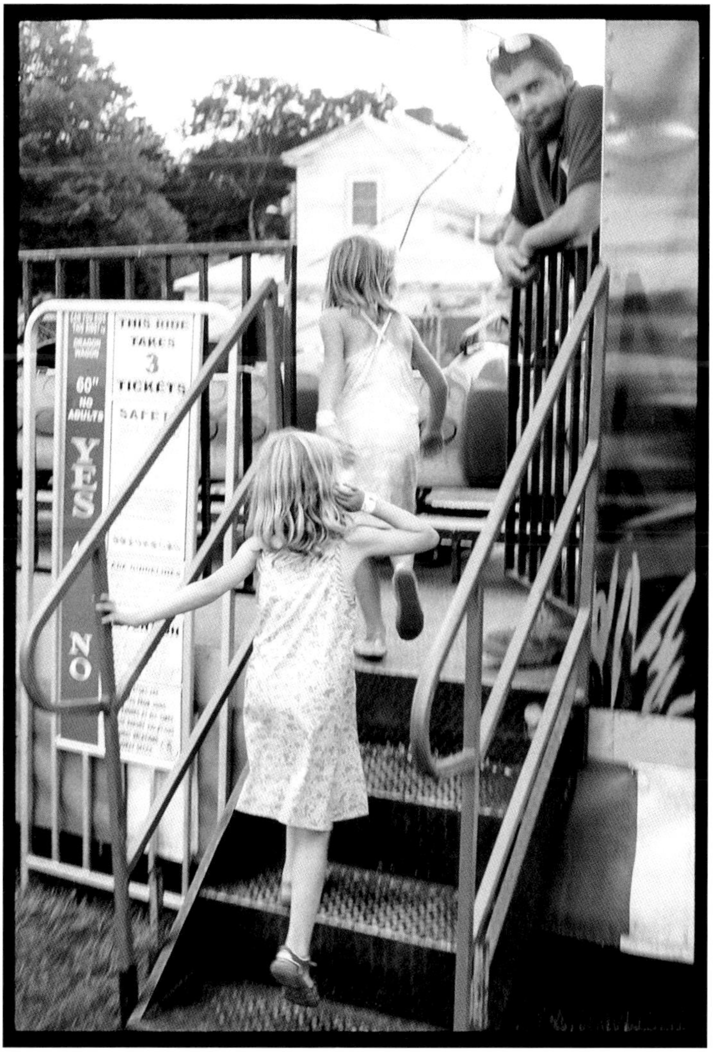

BLURRY GIRLS

RED

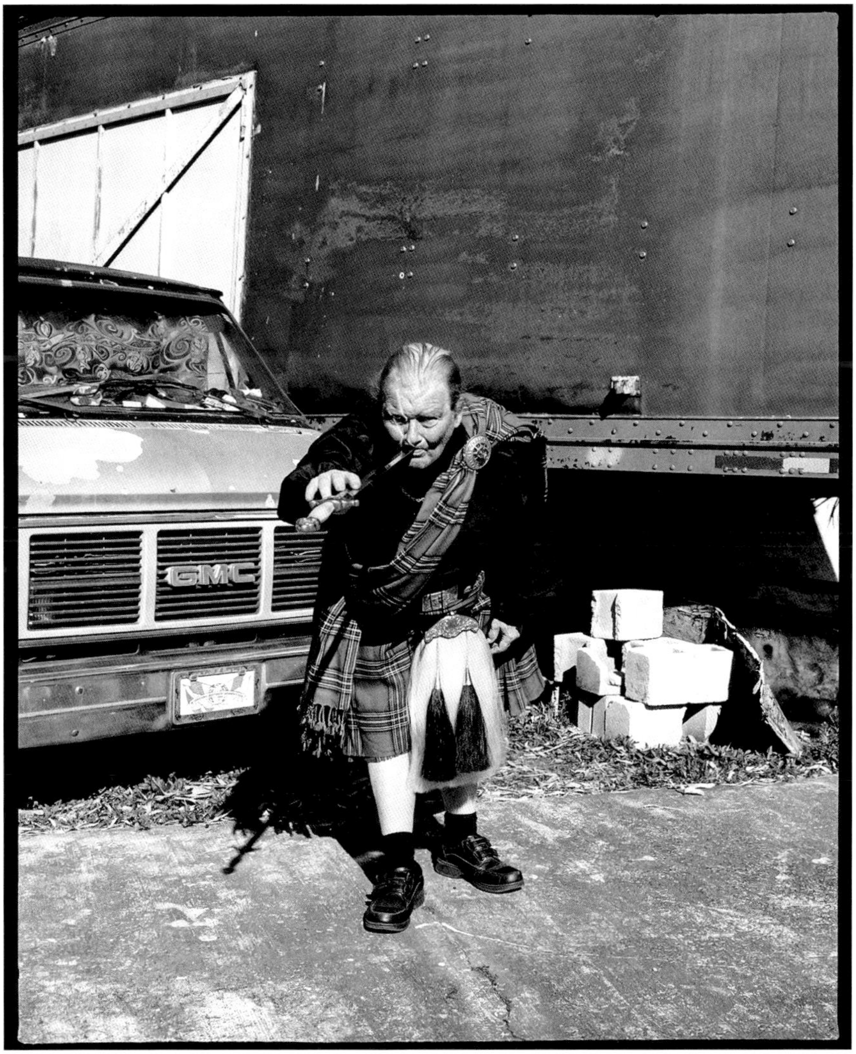
GMC

THE TIGER SHOW

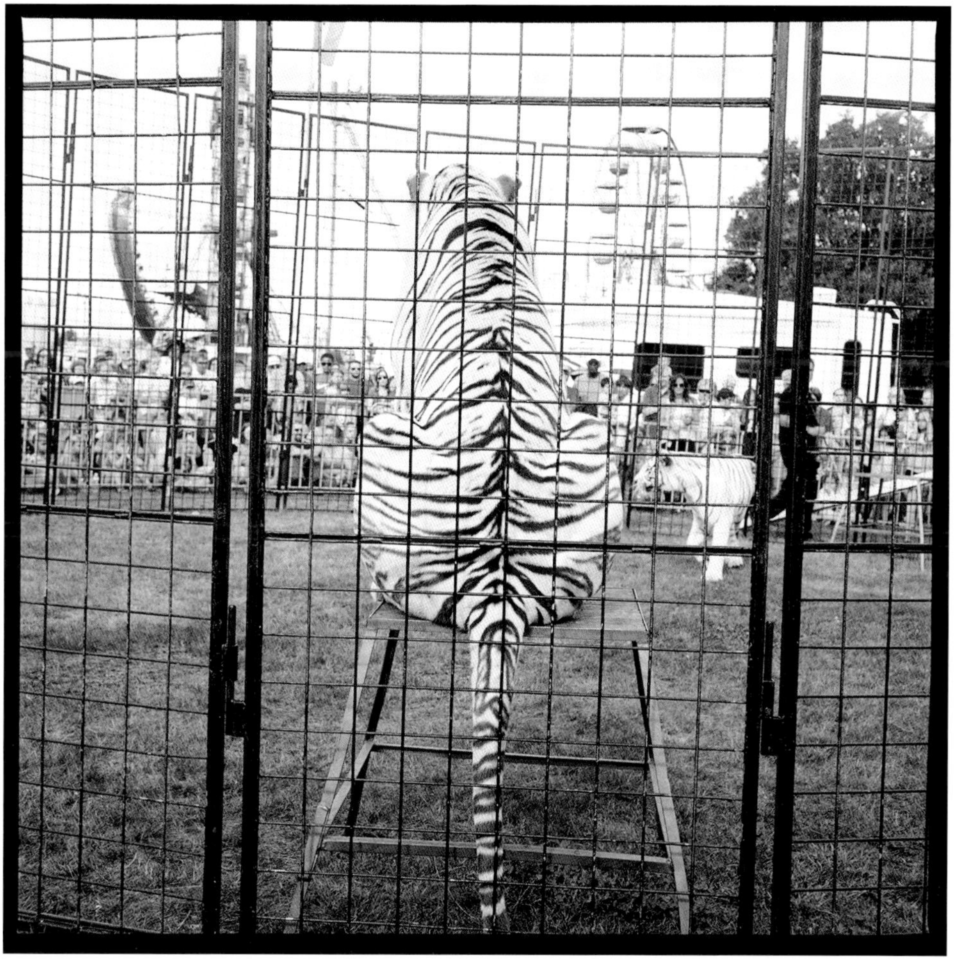

KYZER

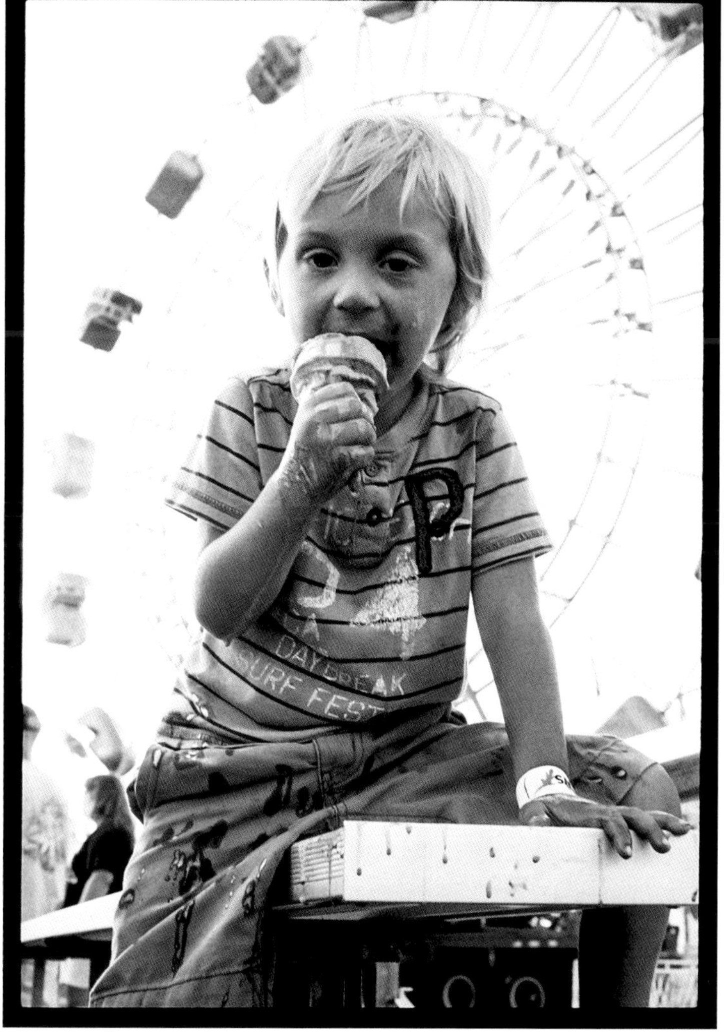
DAYBREAK
SURF FEST

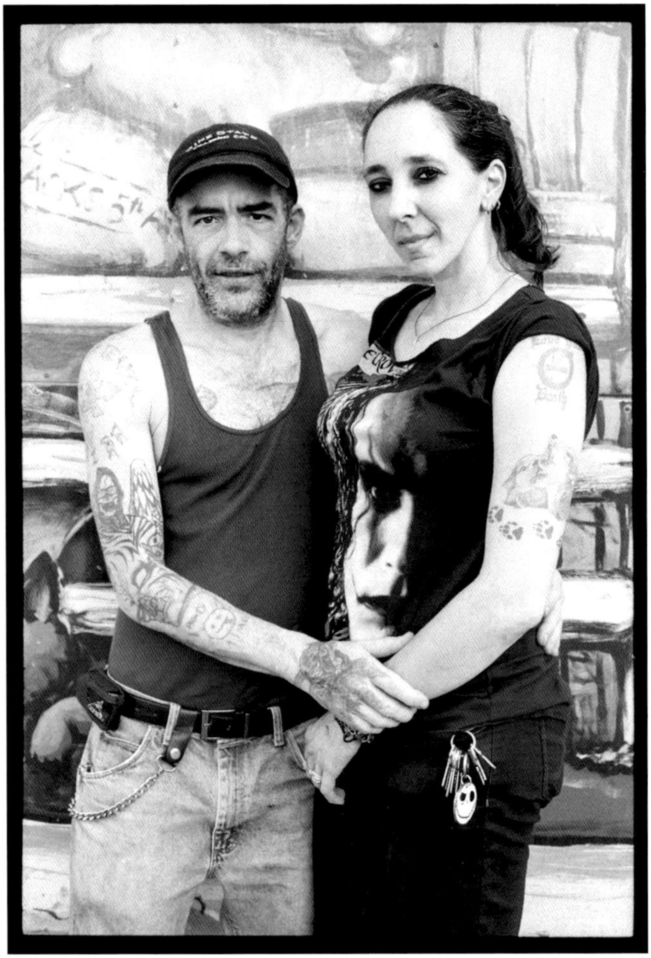

RICK AND ANG

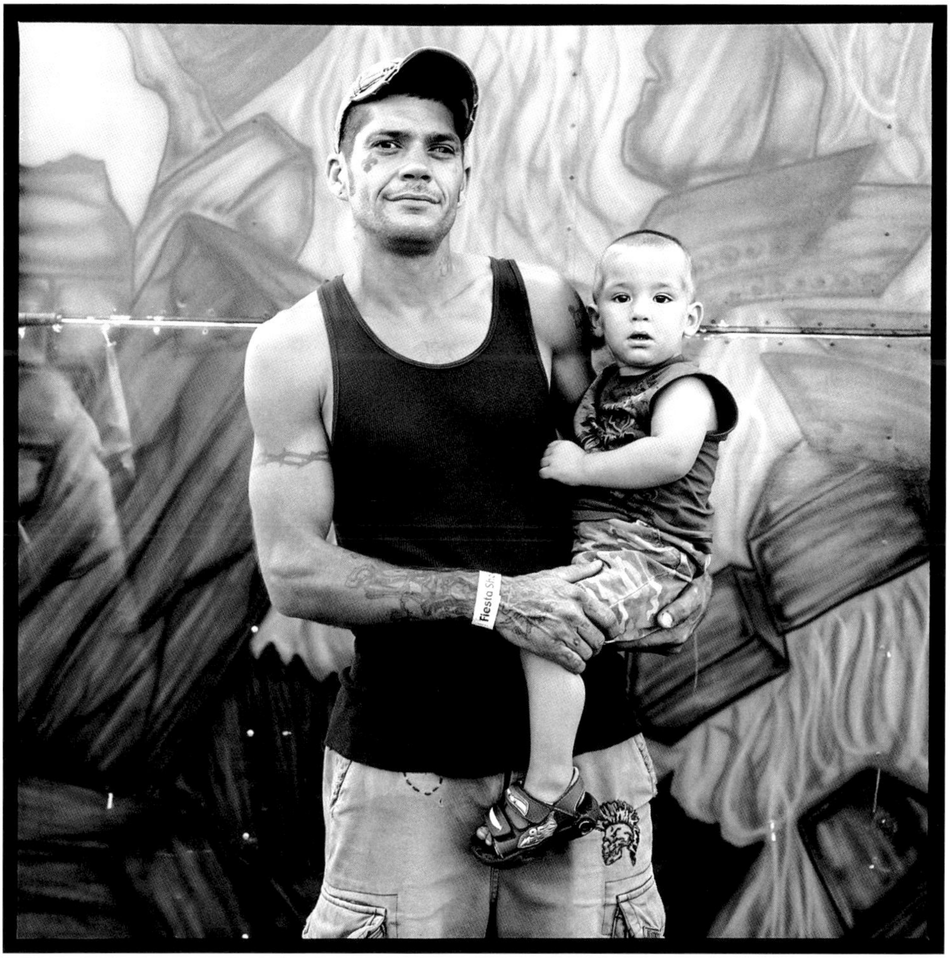

THE FLETCHERS

A DAY AT THE FAIR

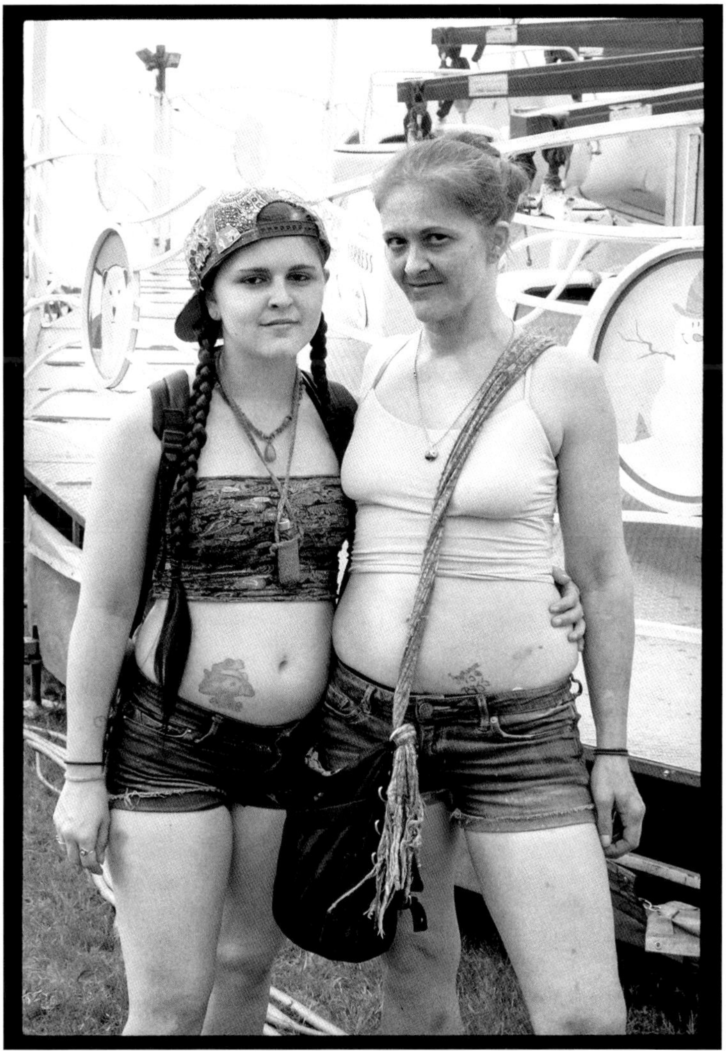

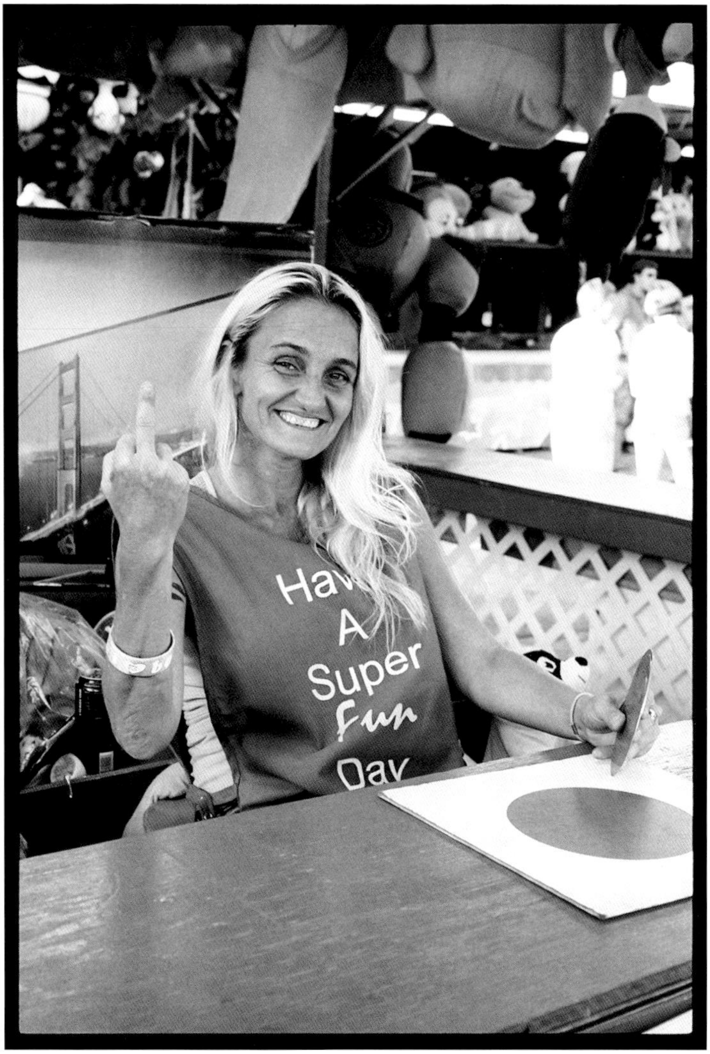

HAVE A SUPER FUN DAY

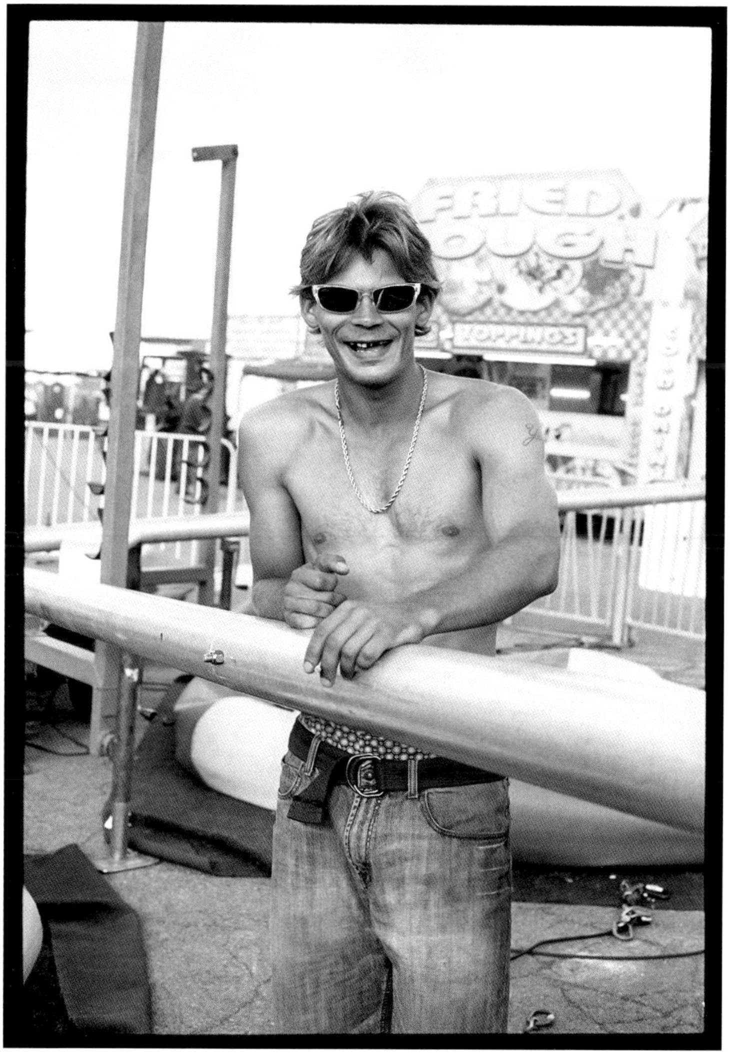

THE BUNGEE GUY

THE CLOWN OF BANGOR

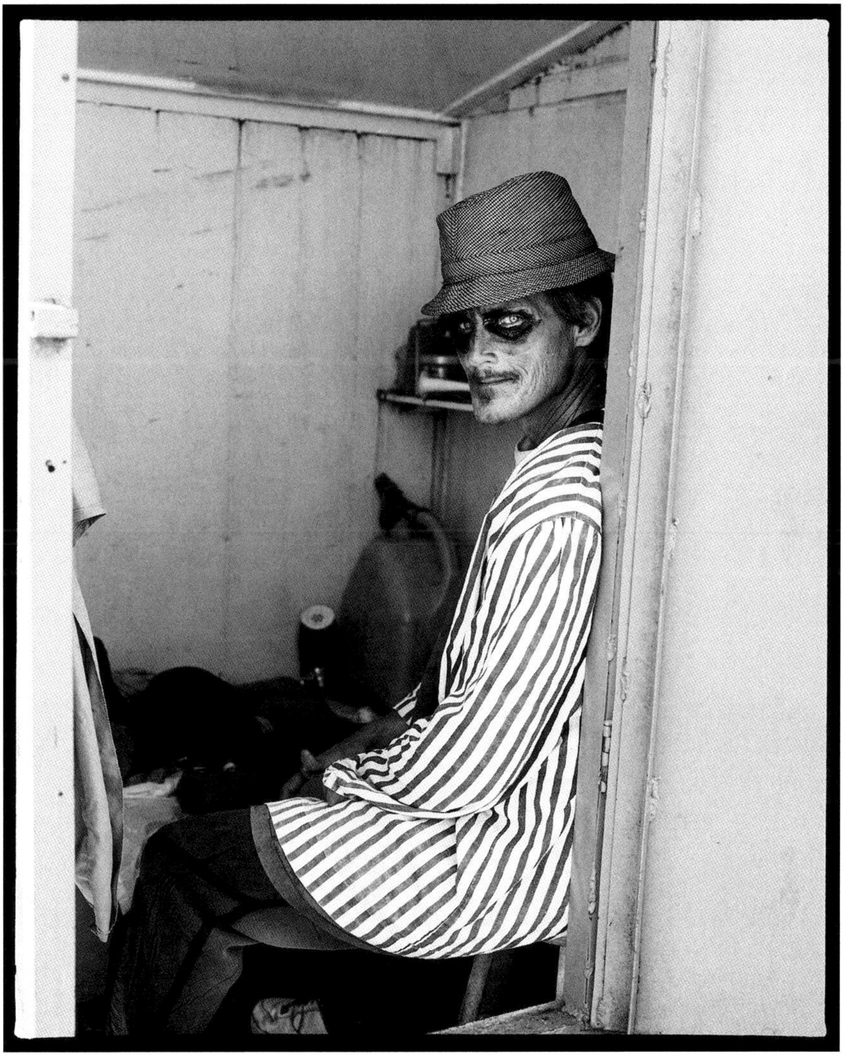

SPOOKY

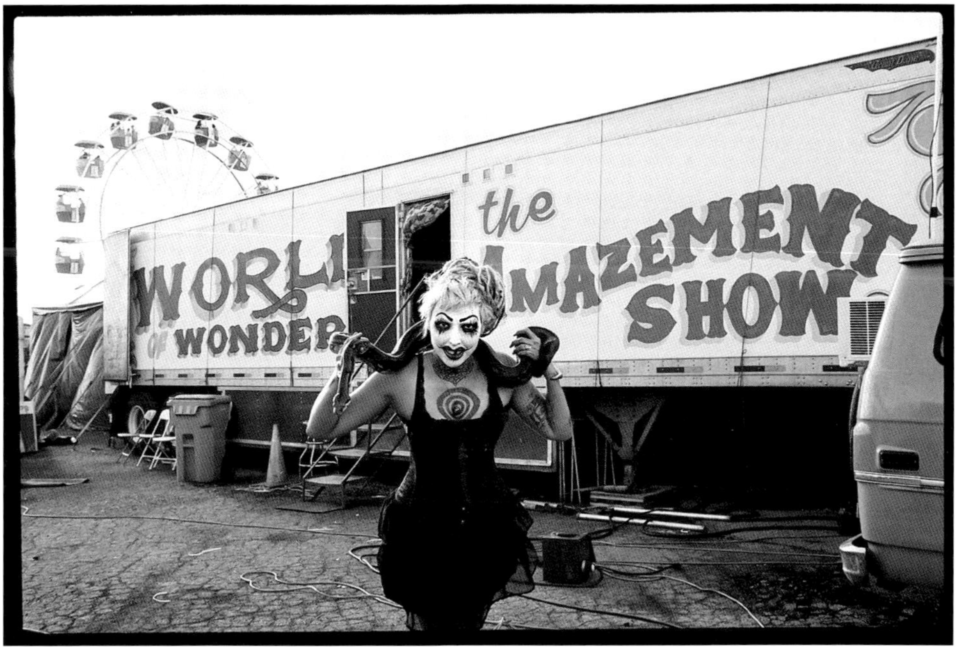

the
WORL
AMAZEMENT
OF WONDER
SHOW

TOMMY BREEN

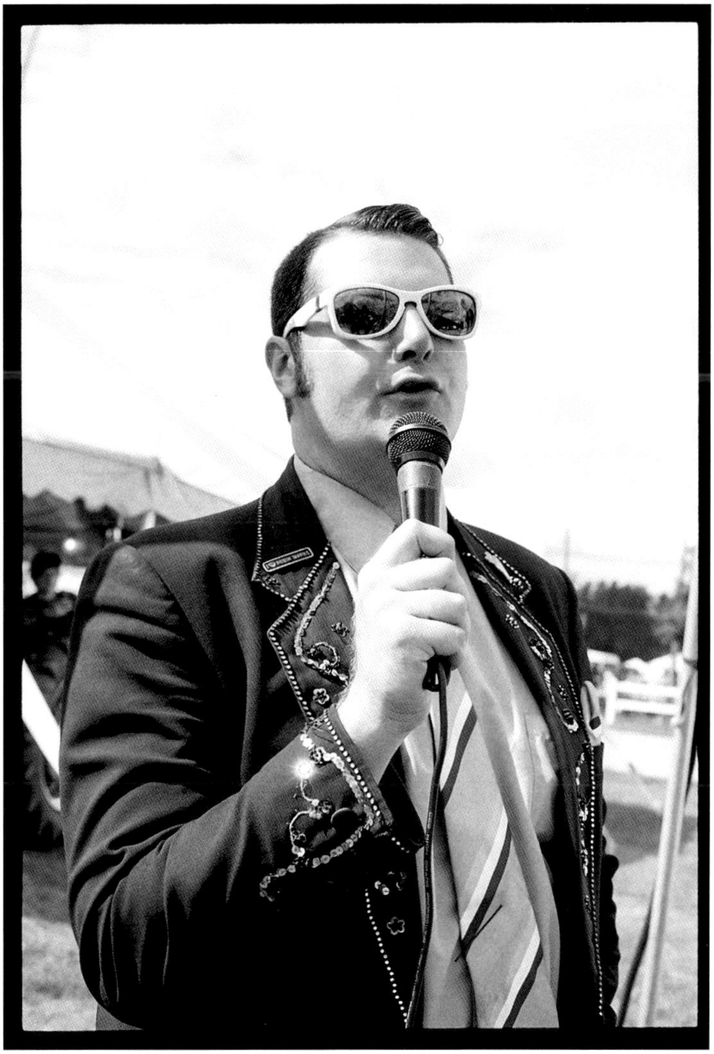

THE ESCAPE EXPLOSION

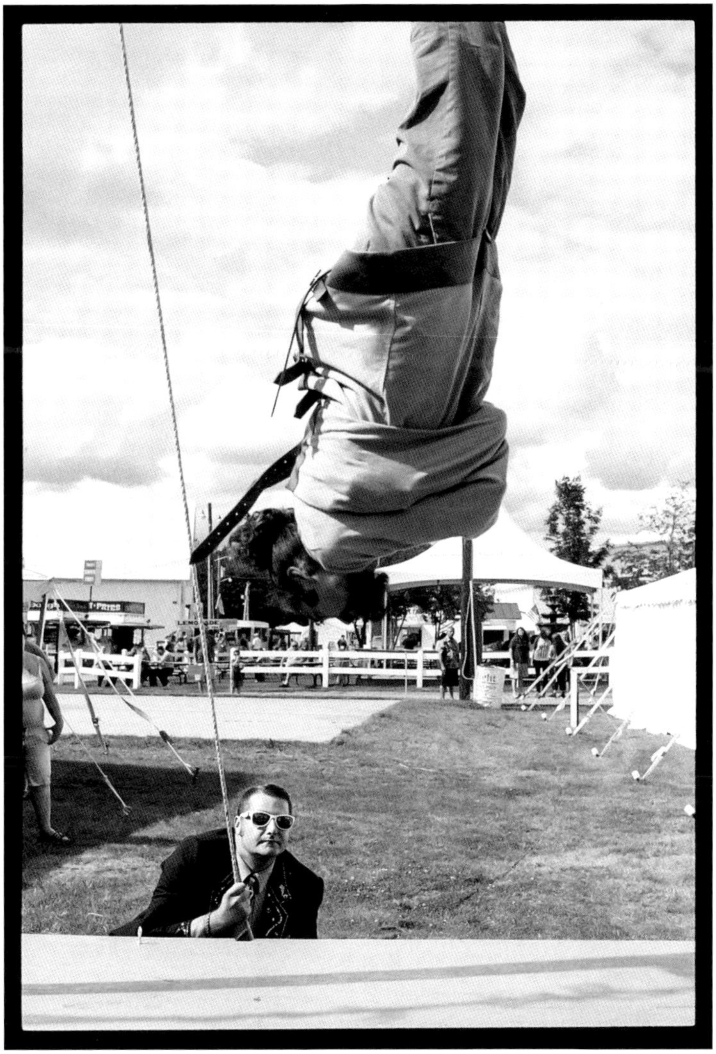

THE LADDER OF SWORDS

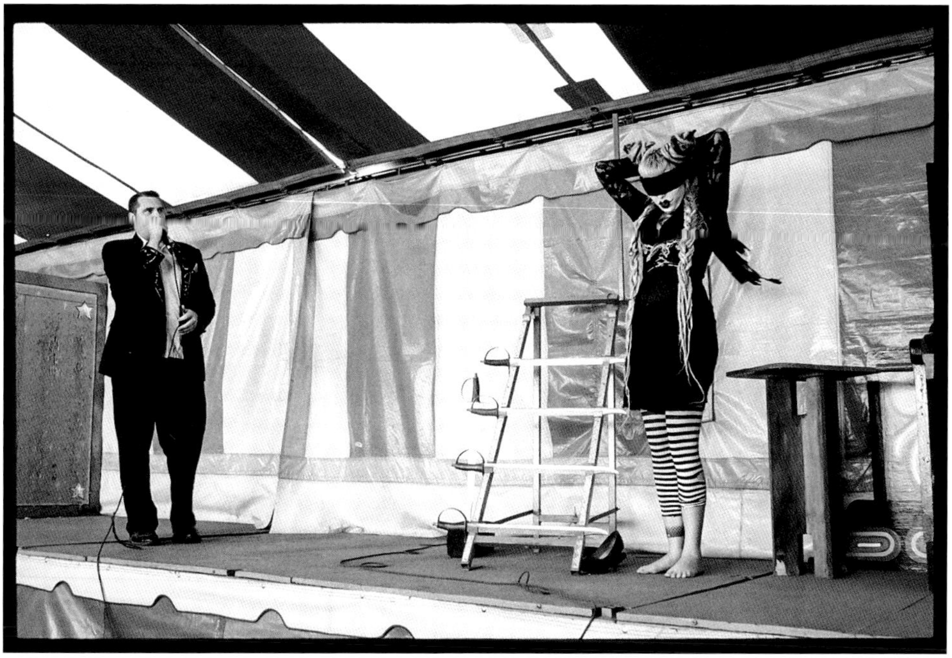

INSECTIVORA

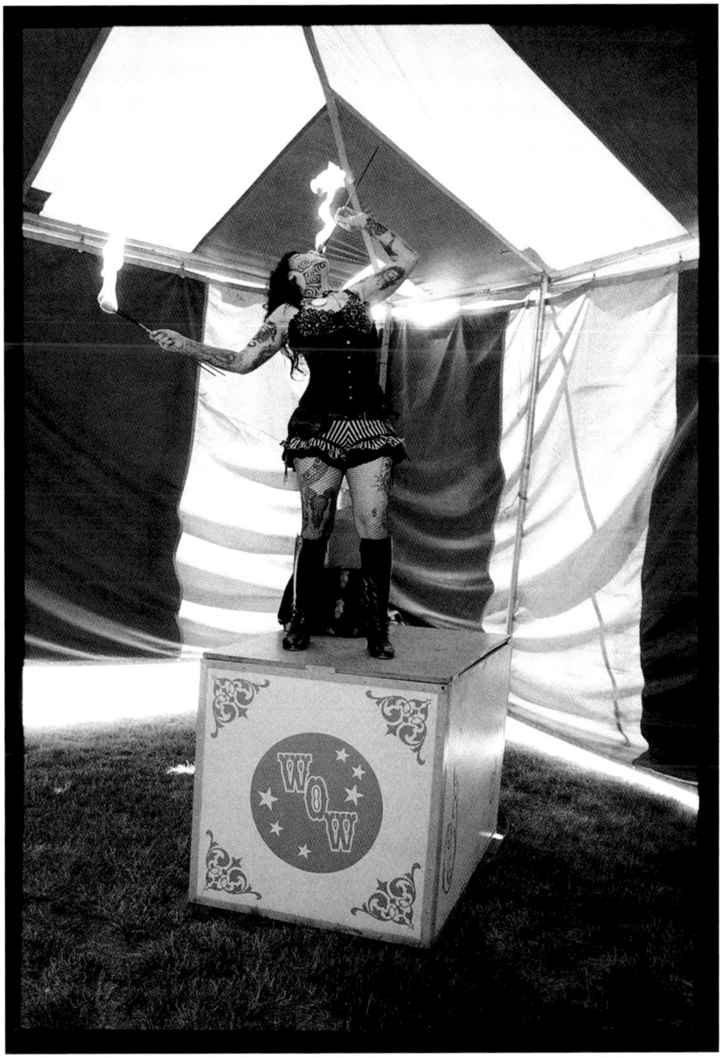
WOW

THE BALLY STAGE

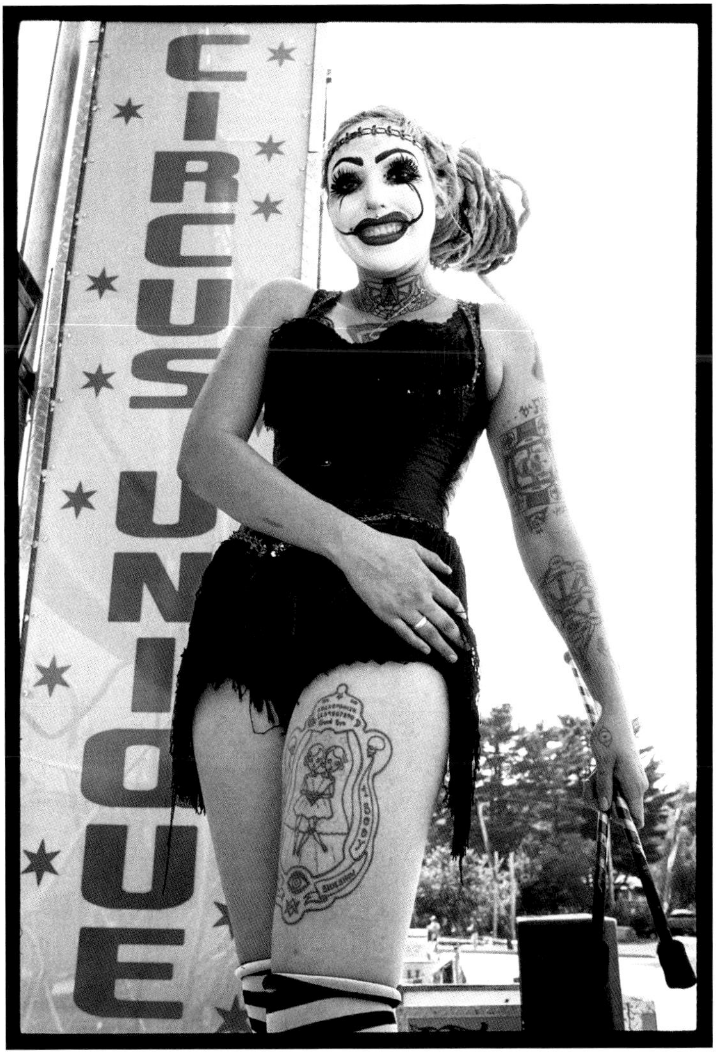
CIRCUS UNIQUE

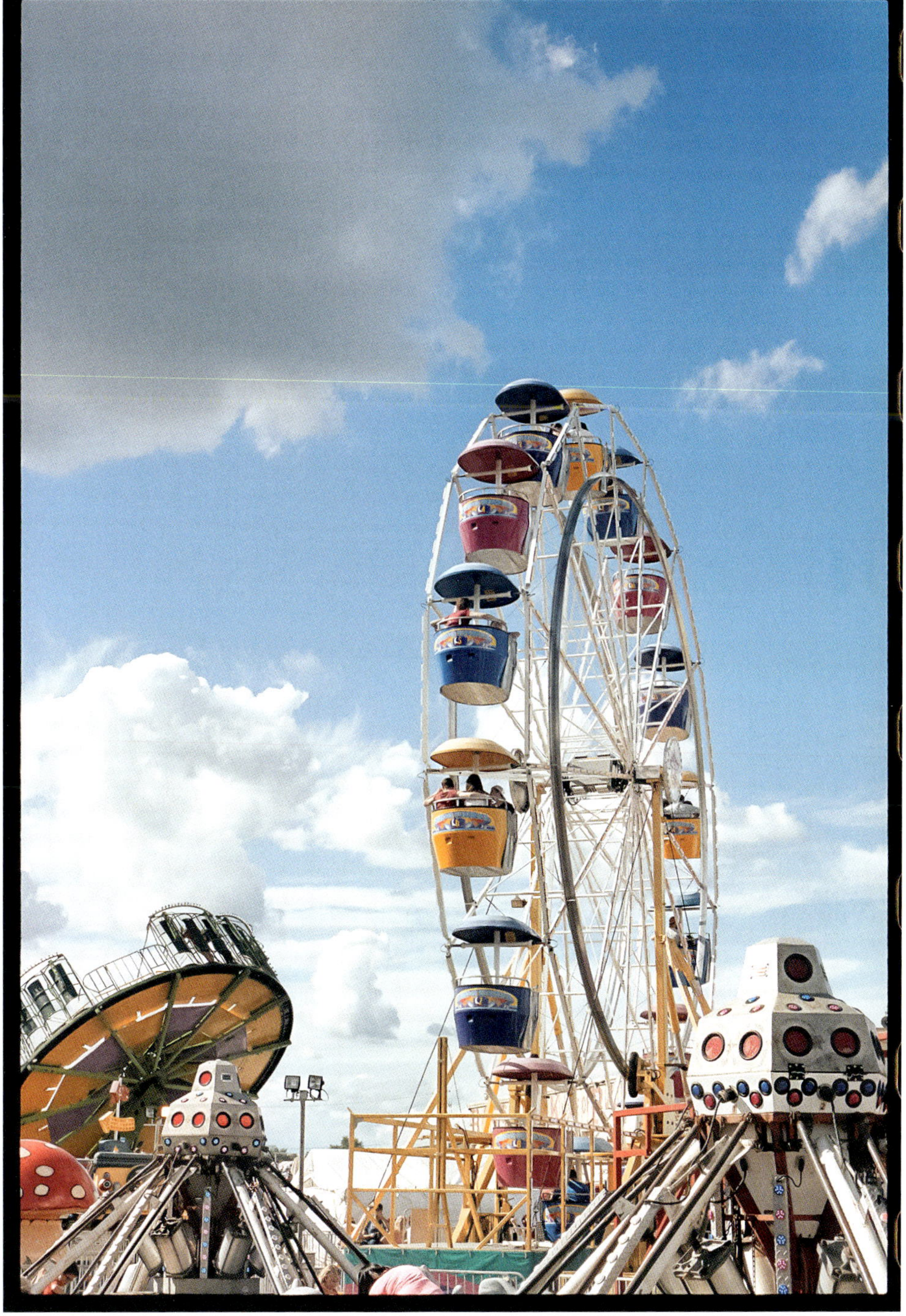

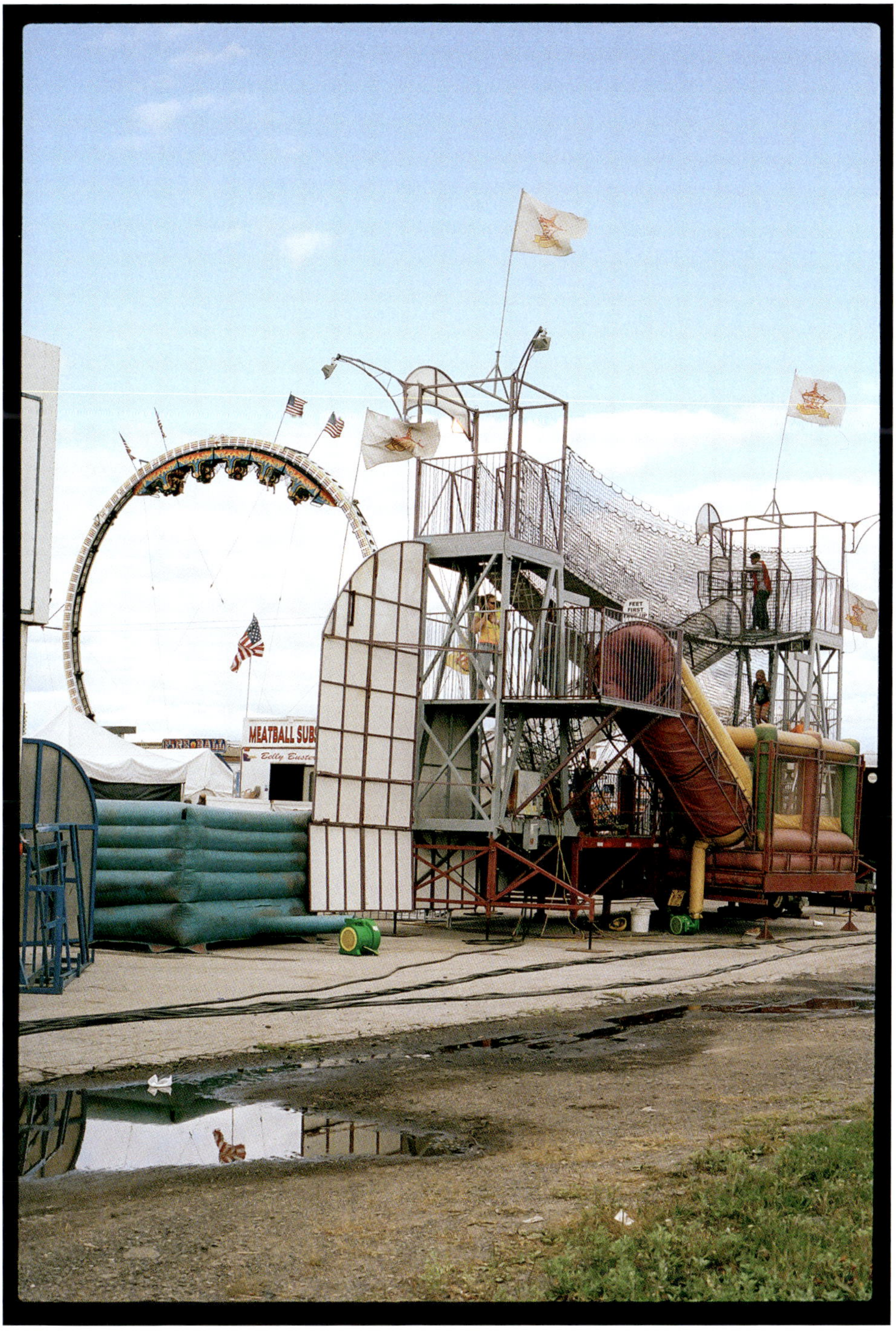
MEATBALL SUBS
FEET
FIRST

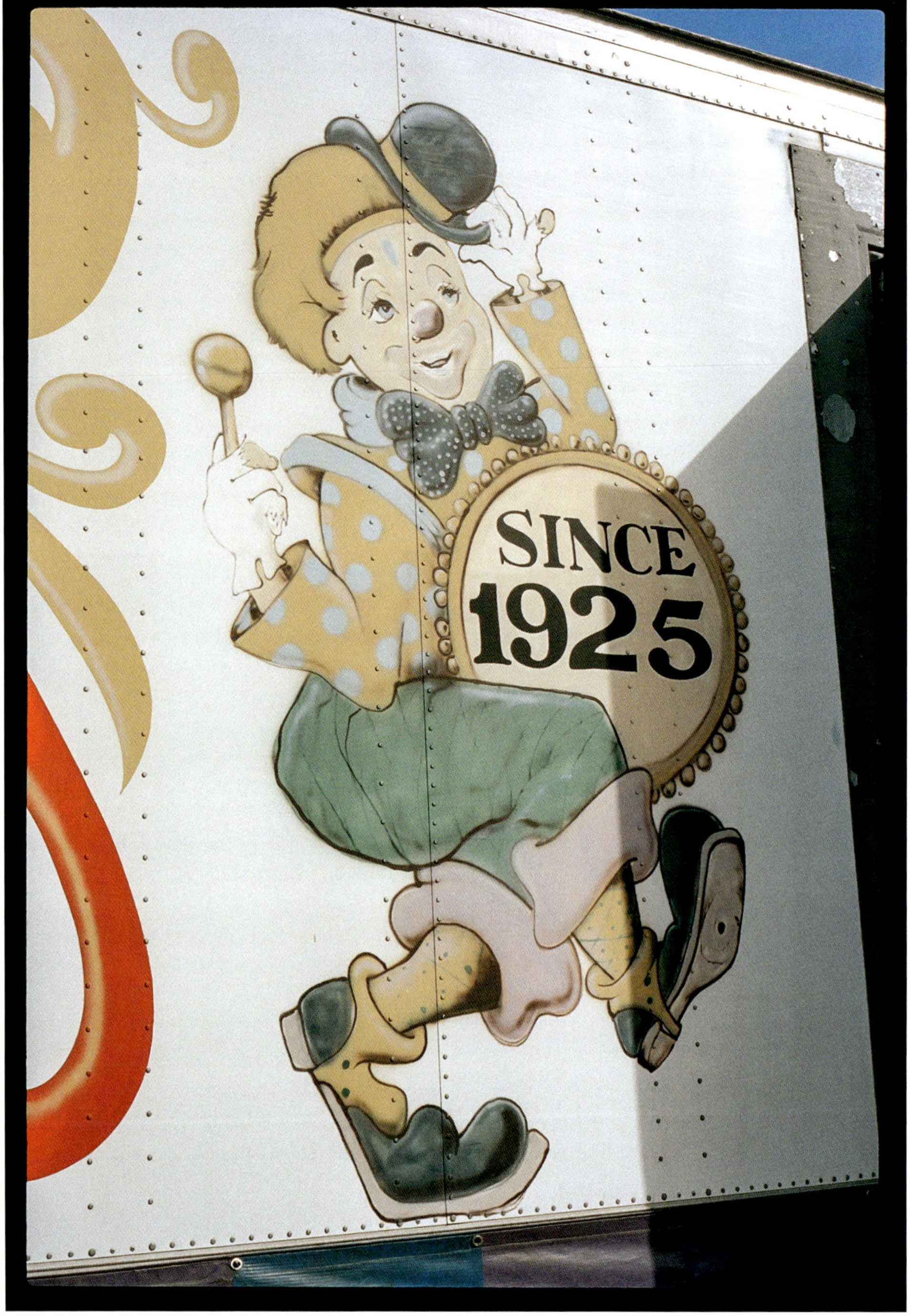
SINCE
1925

ACKNOWLEDGEMENTS

Thank you to everyone in this book, Mom, Dad, my wife Andrea Castagno, Tony Nourmand/Reel Art Press, Mazdack Rassi/Milk Studios, Song Chong/Milk Gallery, Jason Cannon/Milk Velem, Cheyann Benedict, all my family, my brothers and sisters, the Castagnos, Shaun White for the title and cover concept of this book, Ali Elangasinghe and Rory Bruton, Steve Rose, Ward Hall, Red Stewart, Tommy Breen and The World of Wonders.

Nariana Ackley
Zach Adams
Sharon Ainsburg
Josh Ayers
Joseph Baldassare
John Bell
Eric Borgerding
The Chitwoods
John Copeland
Rob Coronel
Dave Damico
Todd and Megan Diciurcio
Alex Hayden
Gibby Haynes
Robert Heist
Michele Hicks
Dave Hill
Lansing Teal Johnson
Charlotte Kidd
Nathaniel Kilcher
Mena Killough
Dylan McDermott
Damien Massingham
Jesse Matthews and Carly Kennedy
Bill and Joanie Matthews
Bob Melet
George Merck
Serena Morton
Nick Newbold
Steve Rifkin/Hank's Photographic
Wyatt Rockefeller
Noot Seear
Michael Schulman
Alice Temperley
Tasha Tilberg
Travis and Liv
Nicole Trunfio and Gary Clark Jr.
Ralph-Jörg Wezorke
Landon Yerby
Alex Yong and Wendy Sturgis

Hunter Barnes
(b. 1977)

Hunter Barnes is one of the foremost documentary photographers working in America today. His photographs document aspects of culture and communities ignored by the mainstream and often misrepresented in the modern American narrative.

Hunter trained in photochemistry and traditional photographic techniques. At a young age, he began a nomadic life on the road. *"For years I've traveled with my cameras capturing moments of time with the people the road has led me to. ... A glimpse into parallel worlds traveling in circular motions."*

In his early twenties, Hunter self-published his first book, *Redneck Roundup*, documenting the dying communities of the Old West. Other projects followed: four years spent with the Nez Perce tribe; months with a serpent handling congregation in the Appalachian mountains; bikers, lowriders, and street gangs; inmates in California State Prison. Intense, true pockets and sub-cultures of America.

The process is an integral part of Hunter's work. He shoots exclusively on film– the pace of analogue in harmony with his approach. *"Certain cameras and film have souls. It's not immediate and has more meaning to me. I have time to develop relationships with the people I'm with. There is a different respect for it, they sit there with you and every shot counts."* Fundamental to Hunter's work is the journey, the people, the place. Then committing them to film before they are greatly changed or gone forever.

Tickets is Hunter Barnes's fifth publication. All his books have been printed as limited editions of 1000. Also available are *Redneck Roundup* (2002) and *Outside of Life* (2004), and from Reel Art Press *A Testimony of Serpent Handling* (2012) and *Roadbook* (2015).

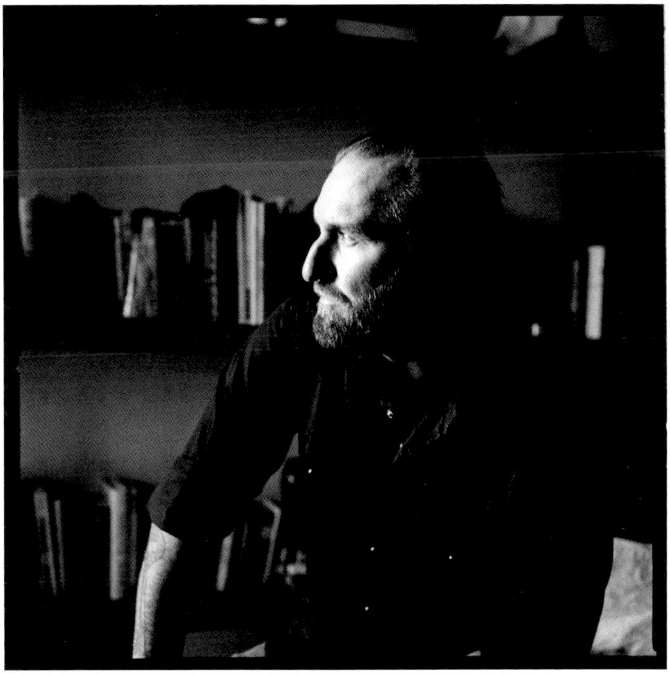

PHOTO: CHARLOTTE KIDD

First published 2017 by Reel Art Press,
an imprint of Rare Art Press Ltd, London, UK

www.reelartpress.com

First Edition
10 9 8 7 6 5 4 3 2 1

ISBN: 978-1-909526-47-1

Edited by: Hunter Barnes, Tony Nourmand and Andrea Castagno
Art Direction and Design by: Joakim Olsson
Project Co-ordination and Text Edited by: Alison Elangasinghe
Image Scanning by : Hass Colby / Velem-Milk Studios

Printed by Graphius, Gent.